KT-386-511

Penguin Education

Penguin Modern Economics Texts
General Editor: B. J. McCormick

Industrial Economics
Editor: H. Townsend

Industrial Concentration
M. A. Utton

Industrial Concentration

M. A. Utton

Penguin Books

Penguin Books Ltd, Harmondsworth,
Middlesex, England
Penguin Books Inc., 7110 Ambassador Road,
Baltimore, Md 21207, U.S.A.
Penguin Books Australia Ltd,
Ringwood, Victoria, Australia

First published 1970
Reprinted 1971
Copyright © M. A. Utton, 1970

Made and printed in Great Britain by
C. Nicholls & Company Ltd, Manchester
Set in Monotype Times

Penguin Modern Economics Texts

This volume is one in a series of unit texts designed to reduce the price of knowledge for students of economics in universities and colleges of higher education. The units may be used singly or in combination with other units to form attractive and unusual teaching programmes. The volumes will cover the major teaching areas but they will differ from conventional books in their attempt to chart and explore new directions in economic thinking. The traditional divisions of theory and applied, of positive and normative and of micro and macro will tend to be blurred as authors impose new and arresting ideas on the traditional corpus of economics. Some units will fall into conventional patterns of thought but many will transgress established beliefs.

Penguin Modern Economics Texts are published in units in order to achieve certain objectives. First, a large range of short texts at inexpensive prices gives the teacher flexibility in planning his course and recommending texts for it. Secondly, the pace at which important new work is published requires the project to be adaptable. Our plan allows a unit to be revised or a fresh unit to be added with maximum speed and minimal cost to the reader.

The international range of authorship will, it is hoped, bring out the richness and diversity in economic analysis and thinking.

B. J. MCC.

Contents

Editorial Foreword

Big business is not simply big; it is out of proportion. This makes it difficult to see large firms in relation to their more numerous, but much smaller, suppliers, competitors and customers. Yet to see them in proper proportion is necessary for understanding industrial organization, operations and standards of performance.

In the last thirty years many efforts have been made to achieve this perspective by measuring industrial concentration. The effort has proved onerous but rewarding as an exercise in measurement, a method of describing industry, and a basis for analysing its performance. This volume sets the problems of measurement in a framework of economic analysis, and applies concentration measurement to economic history and policy.

M. A. Utton became Lecturer at the University of Reading after research work at the University of Glasgow and with the Economist Intelligence Unit. His current research is into mergers in manufacturing and his special field of interest provides appropriate support to this present text.

H.T.

Preface

Industrial concentration within individual industries and within the economy as a whole continually poses problems for the policy maker. Greater concentration, for example, through mergers, is seen by some people as a means of achieving greater economies of scale and faster industrial development, while others would anticipate rising costs and poorer economic performance as a result of the reduction in competition.

The present book sets out the theoretical objections to high levels of concentration but also illustrates the advantages that undoubtedly flow from high concentration in many modern industries. This discussion is extended by a fairly detailed treatment of the factors affecting concentration levels.

Since the whole subject has often been charged with polemics, the strengths and weaknesses of the data and the measures that have frequently been used in empirical studies are discussed at some length. The three central chapters form a survey of the available evidence on concentration levels and trends both in Britain and the United States and are the core of the book. Included are an examination of such questions as whether concentration is higher in Britain than in the United States and whether or not concentration levels in the two countries have shown a persistent tendency to increase throughout the twentieth century.

Before taking up the whole range of policy issues in the final chapter, an examination is made of some of the evidence relating to the behaviour and performance of highly concentrated industries, in particular whether profit levels are significantly higher than in more competitive industries.

I should like to thank my colleagues Professor P. E. Hart and John Mellors for reading through and commenting on an earlier draft of the book. A special word of thanks is also due to my wife who typed quickly and carefully the entire manuscript.

1 Economic Theory and Industrial Concentration

The concern about industrial concentration that economists have recently shown owes its beginning to the development of theories of imperfect and monopolistic competition which took place in the 1930s. One of the propositions which at that time began to be emphasized was the possibility that market imperfections of one kind or another could give rise to patterns of behaviour and performance of individual firms which previously had been associated only with the extreme situation of monopoly. Economists were beginning to stress, in other words, that if relationships existed in the market which enabled some firms to have discretion over, say, their price and production policies, their levels of selling and promotional expenditures and the amount they devoted to research, then the effects usually associated with monopoly could in fact be more widespread in the economy than the number of monopolies as such would have led them to expect. Economists were beginning to emphasize that roughly the same effect can have more than one cause. And with this emphasis came a new difficulty: if the undesired consequences of monopoly resulted also from a nexus which was not strictly speaking monopolistic, how was this expanded problem of monopoly to be solved? Obviously, since the workings of the market were responsible for the problem, the 'solution' heretofore adopted – public regulation, or, as a last resort, nationalization – if now applied to this wider area of difficulty, would entail abandoning the market mechanism altogether. The theories incorporating these discoveries constituted an incentive to detailed empirical investigations of market structures in general and market concentration in particular, and the present text should be viewed against this background.

Although most of the disadvantages of less than perfectly competitive industries could be the result of several forms of market imperfection, the number and size distribution of firms in individual industries are evidently closely bound up with their behaviour and performance. In particular where a high proportion of total industry output or sales is made by a small number of firms, then the industry's performance is likely to diverge considerably from that predicted for a perfectly competitive industry. Economic theory indicates that several important consequences can result from such concentration.

Firstly, where some industries are highly concentrated an optimum allocation of resources is unlikely to be realized. In such industries the price of the product falls as output expands and, in equilibrium, price will be in excess of marginal cost. Even in the long run profits above opportunity cost can persist due to the lack of competition. Compared with an otherwise identical competitive industry, output will be lower and prices higher in an industry of high concentration. For a given level of employment, therefore, fewer resources will be employed in the concentrated industries and more resources in the remaining industries than would have been the case if the economy had been composed solely of competitive industries. As a result, too small an output will be produced by the concentrated industries and too large an output by the competitive industries, causing a reduction in welfare. A primary purpose of the first studies of industrial concentration was, therefore, simply the classification of those industries where output restriction, and consequently a misallocation of resources, seemed most likely to be due to high concentration levels.

Secondly, the lack of competition in highly concentrated industries is likely to affect the internal efficiency of firms. Compare this with the working of a perfectly competitive industry in which the firms pursue profit maximization in the knowledge that inefficiency could lead to their eventual elimination. The monopolists, and to a lesser extent the oligopolists, do not have such a sharp incentive to ensure that the internal allocation of their resources is the most efficient possible. Inefficiency in their case will result in a reduction in profit without the accompanying threat of possible extinction. In addition to the misallocation of resources between industries that occurs as a result of high concentration, therefore, a further misallocation may take place within firms because of their failure to maximize profits.

The third effect which theory predicts will follow from the existence of high concentration, is a change in the distribution of income. Since central Governments have recently made considerable efforts through taxation and transfer payments to change the distribution of income, less importance on grounds of equity is currently attached to this effect than in, say, the inter-war period. Nevertheless the point remains that persistent differences in profit rates between industries because of their structure indicates that a greater share of income is going to the concentrated industries than can be justified on economic grounds. The excess profits are due to the protected position of the firms and they do not fulfill the economic function of inducing increased investment in the industry from new firms.

All three effects described by economic theory clearly refer to the level of concentration in *individual industries*. For convenience, concentration in this sense is referred to below (particularly, for example, in chapter 5) as *market concentration*. It can usefully be distinguished from the idea of *overall concentration* (chapter 4), which refers to the proportion of output or sales in the whole industrial sector, or an important part of it such as manufacturing industry or retail distribution, which is accounted for by a small number or percentage of firms. Concentration in this much broader sense may have important political and social consequences. At about the same time as the theories of imperfect and monopolistic competition first appeared, empirical investigations in the U.S.A. were highlighting the extent to which a relatively small number of companies dominated the entire non-financial sector of American enterprise. The studies also revealed the extent of the divorce of ownership from control which had partly facilitated the enormous growth of joint stock companies but which also meant that effective power over their resources was wielded by boards of directors owning in many cases a minute fraction of the total shares issued.

Some of the inferences drawn from the simple comparison between imperfectly competitive and perfectly competitive industries in economic theory have been widely criticized by writers in the field of industrial concentration. In the first place, it is suggested that in some industries the technological economies of scale are so great that efficient production requires that they be highly concentrated. In such cases if a competitive industry is taken over completely by a few large firms the result is likely to be a greater output and a lower price, resulting from lower costs, than occurred under competitive conditions.

Secondly, it is suggested that the static framework of the analysis and its emphasis almost exclusively on the problem of resource allocation leads it to ignore equally important aspects of industrial performance. Thus it has very little to say about the effect that concentration may have on the rate of technological change. It follows from the assumptions made about perfect competition that knowledge of new products and processes will be quickly spread amongst firms in the industry. But it is possible to argue that for this very reason firms will have little incentive to undertake research and development themselves, since the advantages of any innovation they may make will be quickly diffused amongst their competitors in the industry. Hence Galbraith (1963) argues that the comparative protection afforded to individual firms in a concentrated industry is more likely to encourage them to undertake research and development and thus stimulate technical change.

Both of these issues (economies of scale and innovation) are examined at greater length in the next chapter, which deals with the factors governing concentration levels and concentration change. They constitute the basic dilemma still facing policy makers, i.e. to what extent are the disadvantages of high market concentration in the form of reduced competition and possibly poor resource allocation outweighed by the advantages of scale economies and a rapid rate of technical change? As will be seen in the concluding chapter some of the most recent policy developments in the U.K. have attempted to reconcile these two opposing forces.

2 Factors Contributing to Industrial Concentration and its Maintenance over Time

Introduction

In order to be able to interpret properly the statistical data on concentration considered later, it seems essential to consider first the main factors which influence the level of concentration and its maintenance over time. In view of the importance attached by economists and policy makers alike to the level of concentration it is surprising that there are relatively few systematic discussions of the subject available. (One exception is Bain, 1968, particularly chapter 6.)

For convenience, these factors are discussed below under separate headings, although in practice several of them together may well have played an important part in determining the pattern of concentration in particular industries. The first three sections deal with what might be called 'positive' influences on concentration in that they may improve the allocation of economic resources or increase the rate of growth of output. These are the economies of large-scale plants, the economies of the large multi-plant firm, and research and development and modern technology. In contrast, the last two sections deal with factors whose influence may well be 'negative', by helping to maintain a level of concentration which is not necessarily desirable on grounds either of efficiency or of technical progress, namely barriers to new competition and the inducement to monopolize or cartelize.

Economies of Large-Scale Plant

It has long been an established principle in economics that the technological conditions governing the operation of a single plant in many industries ensure that up to a certain point the average cost of production will fall as output increases. There is little need to describe in detail the sources of such cost reductions in a single factory or technical productive unit since extensive accounts are readily available (see, for example, Edwards and Townsend, 1958, chapter 7, and Robinson, 1959, chapter 2). It is sufficient here simply to indicate the kinds of factors at work.

Best known and most hallowed in economic analysis is the division of labour, which, as it proceeds, allows the quantity of work done by a given labour force to rise. Basically this is a result of the increased skill acquired by each man as he concentrates on a narrow task without wasting time passing from one job to another. At the same time the introduction of specialist machines cuts down the amount of labour involved while making it possible to increase output.

Secondly, there is the set of economies of scale arising from the indivisible nature of many factors of production. For many pieces of capital equipment it is often the case that for technical reasons cost is at a minimum when capacity per time period is high. Consequently only where the plant in which it operates is sufficiently large, with a large output, can the equipment be operated at full capacity and thereby minimize unit costs. Moreover, where such equipment is to be operated as part of a production line in conjunction with others, to obtain minimum costs, the plant may well have to be much larger than the size implied by the output capacity of one piece of equipment considered in isolation. This can be illustrated by a simple hypothetical example. One machine performing a particular operation may have an optimum capacity of 300 units per hour, i.e. costs of production will be lowest when the machine is operated at this rate. If the next stage in the manufacturing process requires the installation of a machine with an optimum capacity of 500 units per hour, unless the plant housing both operations contains five machines of the first type and three of the second, so that the output capacity per hour is 1500 units (i.e. the lowest common multiple of 300 and 500), average cost of production in the plant will not be at a minimum. Any plant smaller than one able to produce 1500 units per hour will have higher average costs than the optimum, since for part of the time one of the machines will be idle.

In some industries the desire on the part of firms to operate plants that are efficient (i.e. operated at their optimum levels) can lead to a high level of concentration. Whether or not this is the case in an industry will depend on two factors: the size of an optimum plant, and the size of the market. Two extreme samples can be used to illustrate this point. In the United States cotton spinning industry an estimate by the U.S. Department of Agriculture (quoted in Weiss, 1961, p. 133) suggested that the most efficient size of mill for producing coarse yarn was one having 10,000 spindles which represented less than one-half of 1 per cent of the total number of spindles in the U.S.A. at that time. It is evident that in this industry the combination of unimportant economies of scale at the plant level and the very large market make possible an industrial structure composed of many plants similar to that described in the model of perfect competition.

At the other extreme we may consider a recent estimate of the size of an optimum plant producing sheet steel in the U.K. According to this estimate (Pratten and Dean, 1965, p. 105), an optimum plant should have a capacity of three million tons per year, which when the estimate was made in 1964 represented 50 per cent of the total U.K. capacity. There is clearly a conflict in this industry in the U.K. between efficient plant size and an unconcentrated market structure. On the other hand, the size of the U.S. market was such that in 1958 it could accommodate sixty-seven plants as large as the Fairless Steel Works built in 1951–2 with a capacity of 2·2 million tons. In the context of the American domestic market, economies of scale at the plant level in the steel industry are quite consistent with a relatively unconcentrated industrial organization.

Two further points should be mentioned when considering the effect of plant economies on industrial concentration. Firstly, in those industries where average costs do not rise sharply in plants of less than optimum scale it may be possible for smaller plants to exist alongside larger competitors without incurring too much of a cost disadvantage. Some estimates made in the early 1950s suggest, for example, that in the United States cigarette industry a plant one-fifth the size of the optimum (which accounted for 5 per cent of the total output) would have costs only 2 per cent higher. In the soap industry costs would only rise 3 per cent for a plant half the size of the optimum (see Bain, 1956, p. 80).

In cases such as these, plants supplying a smaller fraction of the market than one of optimum size may not be at too great a disadvantage to operate successfully and so help to maintain a lower level of concentration in the industry than that implied simply by the size of an optimum plant.

Secondly, in some industries it appears that average plant costs are likely to remain constant over a considerable range of output once the minimum-cost output level has been reached. Thus it may well be possible for a much higher level of concentration at the plant level to occur without loss of efficiency simply because plants are larger than the minimum necessary to obtain the lowest possible average cost.

Economies of the Large Multi-Plant Firm

Where there are further economies open to a firm which grows beyond the scale of the single technical unit and which makes the operation of several plants more efficient than one alone, then it will be necessary to have an even higher level of concentration than that arising out of single plant economies if all firms are to operate on a scale which minimizes average costs.

The factors usually mentioned in this connexion relate to the employment of specialist management, economies of large scale sales-promotion and monetary savings resulting from the large firms' bargaining position (see in particular Robinson, 1959, chapters 3–5). It is possible that some of these reductions in cost may be available to a very large single plant firm. Usually, however, it is assumed that they are only likely to come into effect once the firm has grown beyond the size of one plant.

The scope that a multi-plant firm may have for employing specialists in each area of management to their full 'capacity' is really another example of the economies to be derived from the division of labour and the optimum use of indivisible factors. Thus the very large firm is able to employ specialists in, for example, financial control, market research, sales-forecasting and marketing. Just as in the case of indivisible items of capital equipment, the nearer the factor is able to work to capacity the lower are the unit costs. Simultaneously, further cost reductions are likely to occur in other directions as a result of employing specialists. An accurate sales forecast, for example, can ensure a smoother flow of production and a reduction in inventory costs. Detailed market research may save potentially wasteful research and development effort. The possibility that the multi-plant firm has similar advantages in the field of research and development, and as a consequence is more likely to achieve a faster rate of technical progress, is thought to merit separate discussion and is therefore postponed until the following section.

In those industries where product differentiation is possible and where sales-promotion costs (i.e. costs designed to increase or maintain demand) are an important part of total production and distribution costs, there may be systematic advantages of large-scale sales promotion. By increasing the scale of promotional activities it is possible that firms obtain lower promotional costs per unit of sales at given prices or a higher price per unit of promotional cost. In recent years it has been stressed, for example, that advertising is more effective when conducted through national media (e.g. television) and that increasing saturation of these media will give better results per unit of expenditure.

At the same time, of course, advertising on this scale is only feasible where a large sales volume is assured. These points are illustrated in the following table which relates to the American automobile industry.

Table 1
National Advertising Expenditures (Annual Averages 1954–7) of Automobile Companies

Company	Total expenditure on national time and space	Approximate expenditure devoted to passenger cars	Approximate automobile advertising per car sold
	(millions of dollars)		(dollars per car)
General Motors	106·2	80·7	26·56
Ford	55·1	49·0	27·22
Chrysler	48·5	47·0	47·76
Studebaker–Packard	8·5	7·3	64·04
American Motors	7·9	6·6	57·89

Source: Weiss (1961), p. 342.

Although General Motors' total advertising outlay was much greater than any of its rivals, its costs per unit sold were the lowest. Indeed, to have achieved a comparable advertising coverage, Ford and Chrysler would have had to double their advertising costs per car. Furthermore, if the argument suggested above is correct, the sheer volume of advertising carried out by General Motors makes it more effective in maintaining or increasing demand.

Advantages of a different kind, but no less valuable to the large multi-plant firm, are those stemming from its bargaining position.[1] As a result of its large absolute size it may well receive lower quotations of prices from suppliers of components and raw materials, than a smaller firm. In some cases, of course, this may be due to real economies amongst component suppliers brought about by a larger order (facilitating

1. For a fuller discussion of this point see Edwards and Townsend, 1958, p. 188 et. seq.

better production planning, for example). But in many cases the lower prices may simply arise because the supplier feels obliged to quote more favourable terms to a very large firm which it cannot afford to offend and which may be the source of larger orders in the future. In this case there is no real economy from the point of view of industry as a whole, but naturally the large multi-plant firm enjoys some reduction in its average costs as a result.

It is much easier to describe the possible sources of economies for the multi-plant firm than to quote instances of their precise extent. Only slight evidence is available on the degree to which multi-plant economies may account for a higher level of concentration than that implied by economies at the plant level alone. Economies of large firms do not appear to be so amenable to measurement as those arising at the plant level, where resort can often be made to engineering data which largely governs plant costs.

In one empirical study where twenty manufacturing industries in the U.S.A. were investigated, estimates of the economies of multi-plant firms were available for twelve industries. In only six of the twelve were multi-plant economies thought to be present and then they were considered to lead only to 'small' or 'slight' reductions in average costs. For example, reductions in unit costs as a result of multi-plant compared with single plant operation were estimated to be greatest in the shoe-making and steel industries. But here the upper limit of the cost reduction was only of the order of 4–5 per cent. In the other six industries for which estimates were available no advantages were apparently to be derived from operating at a size greater than one plant of optimum scale. Thus in these cases there was no incentive on grounds of efficiency for concentration to increase beyond that required by plant economies (see Bain, 1956, chapter 3).

In the same study it was found that actual concentration levels in some of those industries where there were no apparent economies available to the multi-plant firm, were considerably higher than the level explained by plant economies. Part of the reason for this may well have been that firms were able to operate several plants of optimum size without materially affecting their average total costs one way or the other. It is then possible for a level of concentration to develop in the industry which is higher than is strictly necessary for plant and firm economies, but which does not in itself lead to inefficiency.

Research and Development and Modern Technology

Few areas of the subject of industrial organization have received more attention or remained more controversial in recent years than that concerning the size of firm and form of market structure most conducive to technological change. Since technical progress is thought to play a significant part in the process of economic growth, which has recently been a primary policy aim in many countries, the importance of the subject is easily explained. The controversy arises from the lack of conclusive empirical evidence.

Two related questions need to be considered in the present context. Firstly, is it now true that in many industries conditions are such that any major technological advance will only come from the very large firm? Secondly, is it also true that whatever the absolute size of firm, a highly concentrated market structure, like those described as monopolies or oligopolies in economic theory, is necessary to give firms sufficient inducement to attempt technological change? Evidently an affirmative answer to both questions would imply that individual firms and possibly governments would have an interest in facilitating industrial concentration.

As far as the first question is concerned it is frequently argued, particularly in connexion with the 'newer' industries such as plastics and electronics, that the absolute size of firms is of paramount importance in ensuring a rapid rate of technological change. Only a firm with large financial resources, it is suggested, can afford to equip and man with highly trained scientists the research laboratories needed by many modern industries. Secondly, large resources are required to set up costly pilot plants for projects which may or may not eventually result in a commercially viable new product or process.

For example, in a recent study of research and development in the electronic capital goods industry, the firms which made a successful transition from the prototype stage to commercial production not only had to combine a well-organized research and development programme with good production planning and efficient marketing but also had to have considerable financial resources.

It was often ten to fifteen years before there was any return on a fairly big investment. Marconi paid no dividend for 13 years; R.C.A. had to wait nearly 15 years for a profit on television and again on colour television. None of the many firms in computers made any profit from them before the 1960s and most of them still do not make any (Freeman, 1965, pp. 40–91).

Thus it is claimed that because the unavoidable and recurrent costs involved in the process of invention, development and innovation are so absolutely high, they form an effective 'threshold' beyond which only the very large firm can afford to proceed.

Most studies that have been made of a cross-section of industries and firms in order to see whether any systematic relationship exists between technical progress and size of firm have had to be content with data on the 'input' side of the process, i.e. resources devoted to research and development, since little systematic data on 'output' in the form of innovation of process or product are available. Broadly speaking the results seem to indicate that (a) just as it is common for large and very large firms to undertake a research and development programme, so it is relatively uncommon for smaller firms to do so; (b) the very largest firms do not appear to devote such a large relative amount of resources to research and development as those regarded merely as large; (c) there is some indication that the cost of gaining new technical knowledge is greater for the largest firms than for those in the large and medium size ranges (see, for example, Schmookler, 1959, pp. 628–32, and Mansfield, 1964, pp. 337–8).

One study which did attempt to investigate directly the relationship between size of firm and innovation in three industries in the U.S.A. did not produce unequivocal support for the hypothesis that the largest firms account for a greater share of innovations than other firms. While it seemed to be true in the petroleum and bituminous coal industries, it was not true of the steel industry (see Mansfield, 1963, pp. 556–77).

In fact to the first general question considered in this section the empirical evidence gives only a very tentative, affirmative answer. Yet when we pass to the second and related question, concerning market structure and technical change, some writers are quite convinced of their case. J. K. Galbraith has argued most persuasively that

the modern industry of a few large firms [is] an excellent instrument for inducing technical change. It is admirably equipped for financing technical development. Its organisation provides strong incentives for undertaking development and for putting it into use. The competition of the competitive world, by contrast, almost completely precludes technical development (Galbraith, 1963, p. 100).

In other words, in the concentrated industry both the resources and the incentive are present to ensure that a rapid rate of technical development takes place. The resources derive from the large absolute size of the individual firms, while the incentive grows directly out of the structure of the industry. In oligopoly, price competition is taboo, but process and product competition are regarded as 'legitimate' by producers, even if the firms receive little head start with their innovations (through inadequate patent protection or close imitations) the small number of firms, and their price behaviour, will at least ensure a partial and fairly prolonged enjoyment of the returns from the development of new products or processes.

In contrast, the firm in a highly competitive industry with no market power is unlikely to see much additional return for any new development it seeks to introduce, since this will be quickly taken up by competitors and, what is more, cost reductions will soon be reflected in a lowering of prices. 'Hence the very mechanism which assures the quick spread of any known technology in the purely competitive market ... eliminates the incentive to technical development itself.' (Galbraith, 1963, p. 101.)

However, the support for Galbraith's hypothesis is by no means unanimous. Vigorous criticism on this point appeared in *The Sources of Invention* (Jewkes, Sawyers and Stillerman, 1958). The authors are especially doubtful about the protection afforded the oligopolist by the abandonment of price competition which thereby acts as a stimulant to competition through innovation. 'The supposed antithesis between price competition and innovation competition is false: they are different forms of the same competitive process. Innovation is competition' (Jewkes *et al.* pp. 168–9). Both on theoretical grounds and as a result of their intensive study of some sixty modern inventions the authors felt that firms in a competitive industry were just as likely to introduce new techniques and products as were firms in more concentrated industries.

Certainly if Galbraith's hypothesis were true, we should expect to find that technical progress had been most marked in highly concentrated industries and, in particular, that industries which have been highly concentrated for some time would show a generous support for research and an outstanding performance in terms of technical progress. It definitely seems true that, for example, in chemicals, petroleum, aviation and electrical engineering high concentration has gone hand in hand with a rapid rate of technical advance. But, on the other hand, examples suggesting quite the opposite can readily be quoted. The aluminium industry in the U.S.A. before the Second World War came very close to the textbook definition of monopoly, and yet its innovation record was unimpressive. The same is also true for the iron and steel industries in both the U.S.A. and the U.K., as well as for other industries which have been dominated by one or a few large firms, such as the case of the British Oxygen Company in the U.K. and the United Shoe Machinery Company in the U.S.A.

The general conclusion of this study was that except for industries with very low levels of concentration where interest in research had been slight and technical advance slow, the picture was too varied to support the all-embracing hypothesis of a systematic correlation between high concentration and rapid technical progress. Nevertheless, for some important industries the requirements of the innovating process are likely to provide a strong force for increasing concentration.

Barriers to New Competition

Once a certain level of concentration has been reached in a particular industry, various factors may act as an effective deterrent to any major change in the level of concentration. Some of these factors are discussed briefly in this and the following section.

In the competitive model of economic theory the possibility of easy entry to the industry by new competition (whether in the form of new firms or firms already established in other industries) helps to ensure that the fragmented structure of the industry, where many firms compete in a market over which individually they have no perceptible influence, is maintained over time. Once the ease of entry is removed then not only is it likely that the market structure will change fundamentally, but also any degree of concentration, once in existence, is likely to remain.

It is evident, for example, from what has been said above about the economies of scale in some industries, that where they are very great in relation to the total market, any potential entrant will have the rather unenviable choice of either entering the industry on a scale which brings him all available cost economies – but thereby so increasing the total supply of output that prices are depressed – or of entering the industry at a scale smaller than the minimum efficient scale for the industry, and thus have unit production costs higher than his more established competitors.

In addition, in industries where product differentiation, and therefore selling costs, are important, a new entrant would have to incur higher selling costs per unit of sales in order to offset the degree of brand preference built up over the years by the past promotional efforts of established firms. Alternatively, he would have to be content with a lower selling price and with unit selling costs only as low as those of established firms.

In the cases described in the two previous paragraphs, and also where established firms have some absolute cost advantage over potential entrants derived possibly from patents or control of essential raw materials, prices can be maintained above the level which would yield a normal rate of return without causing the entry of fresh competitors to the industry. This has important implications for the present discussion. So long as prices are kept just below the level which would induce new firms into the industry (i.e. at a level just below that which would give a 'normal' return to an entrant firm) then the level of concentration is unlikely to change.

The reports of the Monopolies Commission in the U.K. contain several examples of new firms being deterred from entering an industry on these grounds. In a recent report on the manufacture of household detergents the Commission concluded that the past high levels of selling and promotion costs had been an important influence in dissuading new entry to an industry where two firms controlled over 90 per cent of the market. They found it difficult

to see any reason other than that the terms of entry are too onerous, why this profitable field ... should have been left largely in the hands of the two companies. Some of the more obvious potential competitors, such as the large chemical manufacturers are probably not deterred by the mere size of the initial investment required but they may well feel reluctant to participate in – and by participating, perhaps to intensify – the process of competition in promotion expenditure which appears to prevail in the industry (Monopolies Commission, 1966, para. 104).

Advantages from a different source had helped to maintain the dominant position held in the British match-making industry by the British Match Corporation. Through an agreement with a foreign company British Match effectively controlled the supply of match-making machinery in the U.K. Any new entrant to the industry was, therefore, likely to be at a substantial cost disadvantage at whatever scale of operations he chose to operate.

A broader indication of the extent and relative importance of barriers to entry throughout manufacturing industry is given by Bain. Product differentiation appeared from his sample of twenty industries to 'loom larger than any other source of barriers to entry and especially large as a source of high and very high barriers' (Bain, 1968, p. 250). On the other hand economies of scale as an entry barrier, although quite widely found, appeared as an *important* deterrent in only three industries. Absolute cost advantages amounting to a barrier to entry were thought by Bain to play a relatively unimportant role in most industries.

Thus where concentration levels are maintained over time, perhaps even in the face of basic demand or cost changes, the reason will probably spring from some form of entry barrier.

The Inducement to Monopolize or to Cartelize

To the extent that monopolistic power confers on its owner the means of earning high profits, it is to be expected that some firms will attempt to gain such power by, for example, acquiring other firms in the industry. In this case the main drive towards increased concentration does not come from a desire to increase efficiency, as in the case of attempts to derive maximum economies of scale, or from a desire to achieve an improved rate of technical progress. The aim may simply be to gain or keep control of a market in order to earn abnormally high profits or, perhaps, more serious, merely to avoid all competitive effort. According to the Monopolies Commission a policy of this kind had been pursued for some time by the British Oxygen Company, which had attempted to suppress or restrict competition by buying up companies who were competitors in the supply of oxygen and dissolved acetylene (Monopolies Commission, 1956).

Cases of this kind, were, however, relatively rare in the reports of the Monopolies Commission, and in the U.S.A. the anti-trust laws have in recent years effectively curbed the more blatant abuses. It is worth noting, nevertheless, that even in the U.S.A. an effective law dealing with undesirable mergers really dates only from the 1950 amendment to the

Clayton Act, while in the U.K. the Monopolies Commission has only been empowered to investigate certain proposed mergers since 1965. As will be seen later, any tendency for concentration to increase through mergers still causes considerable difficulties to the anti-trust agencies both in the U.S.A. and in the U.K.

Under certain conditions it may be possible for existing firms in an industry to maintain their position and thus the level of concentration by a collusive agreement dealing with such variables as prices, output, retail margins and rebates, and other terms of trading. Most forms of agreement of this kind have been illegal *per se* in the U.S.A. since the passage of the Sherman and Clayton Acts, but in Britain it was left to the Monopolies Commission in the early 1950s to show how effective agreements between manufacturers could be in maintaining the *status quo*. An important category of agreements were those collectively enforced by manufacturers who obtained an undertaking from retailers or wholesalers to sell only their goods. In the Commission's view this was likely to lead to

an excessive rigidity and go far to eliminate possible competition from traders outside the group ... Once a large group of buyers are committed to buy only from suppliers who are members of the group it becomes extremely difficult for any independent producer to find a market (Monopolies Commission, 1955, para. 115).

In this way an agreement among manufacturers can create an 'artificial' barrier to new competition which has an effect similar to those discussed in the previous section.

An agreement of a rather different kind, and one which incidentally was accepted by the Restrictive Practices Court in the U.K. as being in the public interest, seems equally likely to prevent new firms from entering the industry. The agreement set prices in the cement industry at such a level as to ensure a 'satisfactory' rate of return for existing firms, although the rate seemed to be somewhat below the average for manufacturing industry as a whole. Existing firms were satisfied with the relatively low profit rate since, they claimed, risks were reduced through the maintenance of the agreement. However, since the rate of return was kept artificially low potential entrants were unlikely to be induced into the industry. In this case the established firms seemed to be purchasing 'a quiet life' at the cost of a lower rate of profit.

Conclusion

The previous sections have outlined some of the more important factors influencing the level of concentration in industry. They should not be considered exhaustive nor should it be concluded that there are no forces working in the direction of a decrease in concentration. Opinion is by no means unanimous that the natural tendency in capitalist economies is to an inevitable increase in concentration (see, for example, Blair, 1948, pp. 111–52). Also the later discussion of the statistical data on concentration will bring out that it is by no means certain that concentration has on the whole increased, at least in the U.S.A., over the last forty years or so.

One general factor working against an increase in concentration, particularly since the last war, has been the largely sustained growth in demand. In such conditions firms established in particular industries will have to increase their own sales as fast as total industry demand is increasing, if the level of concentration is not to fall. It is also clear from the studies mentioned in the above discussion that the impact of the various factors on industrial concentration has not been uniform throughout industry. Economies of scale, for example, have played a much greater part in influencing the level of concentration in the British petrochemicals industry than in the production of nylon where patent rights have played a large part. Furthermore different factors have been of importance at different times. Compared with seventy or so years ago, when increases in concentration occurred through the formation of 'trusts', often with a monopolistic purpose, the needs of research and development in some industries now seem to be a much more significant influence.

3 Measures of Concentration

Introduction

The purpose of the present chapter is mainly methodological. Its aim is to describe the kinds of measures of concentration that have been used in empirical studies, why they have been used and what their shortcomings are. It can therefore be regarded as an introduction to subsequent chapters, which present a survey of the statistical evidence available on concentration.

An important distinction was made in chapter 1 between overall and market concentration. Concentration within the economy as a whole or in a broad subsector of the economy, such as manufacturing industry, will be termed *overall concentration*. Studies of concentration in this sense have typically focused attention on the position of the largest 100 or 200 firms in the economy and in separate industrial sectors.

The expression *market concentration* will refer to concentration within individual markets or industries, in particular the proportion of total industry output produced by the largest three or four firms. In practice considerable difficulties surround the measurement of market concentration and these are discussed below.

It does not necessarily follow that a high level of overall concentration is inevitably accompanied by a similar concentration level in individual industries. If, for example, the largest firms in an economy are extremely diversified while the industries in which they operate are large, then it is possible for high overall concentration to exist side by side with relatively low market concentration. It should be evident that the reverse case is also possible.

A second important distinction concerns the *concept* of concentration that underlies the particular measure used. Many studies have measured the proportion of total assets or sales controlled by a small *number* of very large firms, either in the whole economy or a single industry. These will be termed *absolute* concentration measures in the subsequent discussion, and it will become clear below that confusion can arise if absolute measures are not clearly distinguished from *inequality* measures. The latter consider the *percentage* of the total number of firms in the economy or an industry that control a certain percentage of total assets or sales.

The Measurement of Market Concentration

The need to measure market concentration grows directly out of price theory which suggests the possibility of the misallocation of resources and income where markets contain strong elements of monopoly or oligopoly. A measure which highlights in an economy those industries where these dangers seem most likely to arise would provide a useful preliminary framework for public policy in the field of competition and monopoly. Where the industry actually observed bears a close resemblance to the industry of economic theory, market concentration measures could also be useful in predicting the behaviour and performance of industries. However, the available statistics of individual industries that are frequently used in the measurement of industrial concentration are far from ideal and raise considerable difficulties of interpretation.

From what has already been said about the concept of an industry and a market in economic theory, it is evident that the statistical data used should ideally be grouped so as to give industries which include products having either high cross-elasticity of supply or high cross-elasticity of demand.

The industrial groupings most commonly used in the

compilation of market concentration measures are those given in the Census of Production in the U.K. and the Census of Manufactures for the U.S.A. The delineation of industries or trades in these publications is usually based upon the concept of a group of 'principal products' which is determined mainly from the side of supply, in particular from the prevailing technological conditions. For example, it is common for the group of principal products for an industry to be determined by their use of the same raw or semi-processed materials, or because they are worked upon by the same kinds of processes. The basic unit for the collection of data in the Census is the *establishment* which amounts to a single productive unit such as a plant, factory or mine at a certain geographical location. The term *enterprise or business unit* refers to the company or corporation including all of its subsidiaries. Obviously many business units will own more than one establishment and the possibility that these may be operating in different Census industries leads to complications in the use of concentration data which are referred to again below.

Once an industry has been defined in terms of a group of principal products then the establishments included in the industry will have a greater part of their output consisting of these principal products than those of any other group. It is evident that building up industries in this way is likely to lead to a considerable divergence between the industry of the Census and the kind of theoretical industry ideally required for a study of market concentration. Although it is quite possible that in some cases the outputs of establishments using, say, the same raw materials may manufacture products which have a high cross-elasticity of demand it is equally likely that the products are far from being close substitutes and therefore strictly speaking do not belong to the same industry. To include in the same industry, for example, all establishments whose main activity is manufacturing rubber products would mean that the industry's output may include such diverse items as rubber tyres and tubes, rubber foot-wear and rubber for furnishings. To limit this difficulty it may be possible to use a finer classification by breaking down rubber tyres and tubes and rubber footwear into two separate industries. However, in the case of rubber footwear this only serves to highlight another difficulty. It is quite evident that rubber footwear is a close substitute for footwear made of other materials but this output will have been classified as belonging to another industry – in the case of the U.K. Census of Production, to the distinct 'footwear' category. In short, industries in the Census based on the idea of 'principal products' which are grouped mainly according to conditions governing supply may either *include* products together in the same industry which are not in direct competition or *exclude* products which are really close substitutes for the industry's output.

It was mentioned above that establishments are allocated to Census industry X if the greater part of their output consists of the 'principal products' of industry X. But in an extreme case it would be possible for an establishment with a very diverse output to have only a relatively small proportion consist of the principal products of industry X and yet because no other group of products has a larger share of the total, the whole of its output is included in industry X. Evidently if many establishments of this kind occurred a large proportion of the apparent output of industry X would really consist of products more strictly belonging to other industries, and any concentration ratio calculated from such an industry would have little meaning. In detailed studies of industrial concentration (see, for example, Evely and Little, 1960), it has been possible to test the success with which Census planners have been able to avoid this shortcoming in their industry groupings by calculating the 'degree of specialization' and the 'degree of exclusiveness'. A high degree of specialization by an industry means that a large proportion of the total output of the Census industry was composed of the principal products for that industry (implying that establishments included in the industry were highly specialized). Similarly a high degree of exclusiveness would mean that a given set of 'principal products' was produced to a large extent in the industry for which it was designed. Thus if an industry has 100 per cent degree of specialization and exclusiveness this would mean that all output of the industry was composed of the industry's principal products and also that the total output of the industry's principal products occurred in the appropriate industry. By eliminating those industries which have low degrees of specialization and exclusiveness a closer approximation can be made to concentration ratios which represent the level of concentration of a known group of principal products.

Apart from these difficulties, which really arise from the attempt to use Census material for the analysis of a subject for which it was not principally designed, various other problems are associated with the use of concentration ratios as indicators of market structures close to those postulated in economic theory. An important source of over-statement of the level of concentration, for example, may arise by not taking into account a level of imports high in relation to domestic output. Without adjustment, a concentration ratio based simply on domestic output (which is all that is included in the Census of Production) might give a misleading impression of the true level of concentration in the industry.[1] In the opposite case, of course, the competitive conditions in the domestic market may be substantially different from that indicated by a concentration ratio based on domestic output if a high proportion of the output of an industry's largest producers is exported. In this case again the concentration ratio would tend to overstate the actual level of concentration in the domestic market.

A further source of over-statement of the actual power

1. However, import information used to modify concentration ratios should be used with care. Evely and Little cite the example of the import of matches into the U.K. in 1949–50. This amounted to 38 per cent of total domestic sales and on the face of it appeared to modify considerably the dominant position held by the British Match Corporation which was then responsible for 87 per cent of sales of home produced matches. In fact because the British Match Corporation was also responsible for 89 per cent of imported matches its position was strengthened rather than weakened by the existence of imports (Evely and Little, 1960, p. 46).

of the largest producers in an industry which seems to be highly concentrated may derive from the existence of countervailing power on the other side of the market amongst buyers of the industry's products. Galbraith (1963, p.118) has suggested that for the U.S.A. the emergence of highly concentrated buying groups has in effect neutralized the opportunities to exploit a monopolistic or concentrated oligopolistic position which has grown up amongst producers. As an illustration from the U.K., Evely and Little (1960, p.47) cite the case of the costing done by the General Post Office of submarine telegraph cable which was produced in the U.K. by a single company.

On the other hand, however, various factors make it more likely that high concentration ratios will tend to *understate* possible levels of monopoly power. In the first place for Census purposes an enterprise is taken to control another company if it has a greater than 50 per cent holding of the latter's equity capital. At least since the study by Berle and Means (1932) of ownership and control among large American companies in the early 1930s it has been recognized that *de facto* if not *de jure* control of another company can arise where there is a wide dispersion of equity shareholdings, with a holding of far less than 50 per cent. Thus an enterprise recorded by the Census as big enough to figure amongst the largest three or four in an industry may well in fact have control over a larger proportion of total industry output by virtue of its minority controlling interests in other companies. To the extent that this occurs amongst the largest enterprises the recorded concentration ratio will understate the actual position.

A similar and related source of possible understatement may arise from vertical integration amongst large companies. Different plants of the same firm carrying on production at various stages in the industrial process can mean that they will be included individually in several different industries in the Census. The output of an individual plant will be included in the calculation of the total output and the concentration ratio for the relevant industry, but the fact that the plant is only part of a large vertically integrated concern may well mean that it can exercise considerably more influence over the behaviour of its particular market than would appear simply from the size of its output. This is likely to be particularly important where the integrated concern is large enough to act in one phase of its operations as a raw material supplier and in a later phase as a competitor with the same firms. It may thus be able to charge high prices for the raw materials while deliberately cutting margins on its own final products in order to 'squeeze' its competitors. Evidently market pressures of this kind, a function of vertical integration cannot be reflected in the concentration ratio.

An equally important source of understatement in a country the size of the U.S.A., but probably less significant in one as compact as the U.K., is the size of the market and transport costs. As far as the Census is concerned the data on individual industries are given for total domestic output. For purposes of economic analysis bearing on the degrees of monopoly and competition, the market may be considerably smaller than that implied by total output in the whole economy. High transport costs, especially where the product is bulky and has low value per unit of weight, may mean that the market is composed of several regional areas within which some producers may enjoy a large amount of monopoly power. This may occur even though concentration for the whole economy is relatively low. Considerations such as these led Kaysen and Turner (1959) in their classification of market structures in the U.S.A. to distinguish national from local and regional markets for which separate concentration measures could be calculated.

The number of possible limitations that have been put on the use of Census material for measuring concentration in individual markets may seem to leave very little scope for its positive application in the empirical analysis of monopoly and competition. These qualifications are undoubtedly important and must be borne in mind if a correct appraisal of their use in statistical studies is to be made. But as one leading student in this field has suggested, it is sufficient that the concentration measure 'can point to the existence of markets in which the presence and effects of oligopoly deserve detailed study; no more sophisticated measure calculable *without* such detailed study of the particular market can do any more. (Stigler, ed., 1955, p.117). This point can now be taken up more directly by consideration of those measures that have been employed in the study of concentration.

Concentration Concepts and Measures

At this point it is convenient to mention the choice between various possible ways of measuring sizes of plants and firms to calculate concentration levels. Frequently, as many as four different economic quantities may be available: sales, value added, employment and assets. The difference between the first two, both of which for example are given in the U.K. Census of Production, is that sales are simply the total receipts from the sale of the firms' products, while value added is the difference between the sales figure and the cost of such purchases as raw materials and fuel and power. For present purposes value added is preferable to sales. Two firms may have the same percentage of total industry sales, but whereas one may undertake the whole process of production the other may only purchase and assemble components made by other firms. In terms of resources employed in the industry and the implications for economic efficiency, therefore, the first firm is much larger than the second. But this suggests that either assets or employment may be better magnitudes for use in the measurement of concentration. Here again, however, there are difficulties. There are good reasons to believe that a measure based on capital would tend to overstate, and one based on employment to understate, the actual level of concentration. Large firms are likely to be more capital intensive than small firms since the scope for labour saving machinery in many industries tends to increase with size.[1] It is also possible that large firms may be in a position to obtain better terms from suppliers of machinery than small firms. On the other

1. See chapter 2 particularly the first section.

hand there is considerable evidence (for example, Bates, 1964) to suggest that a major inhibiting factor on small firms is their limited access to financial capital, whereas for large firms constraints on their growth come from other sources.

Furthermore, the nature of the available asset figures may limit their use in the measurement of concentration, particularly where comparisons between different points in time are to be made. The difficulty here stems from price changes and the valuation of assets. A company's assets at a particular time reflect an accumulation built up over a considerable period. The time pattern of asset purchases will almost certainly not be the same for companies in the same industry and if there have been substantial changes in prices, assets will not be strictly comparable as between companies. There is also likely to be some variation amongst companies in their methods used for valuing existing assets, which may not only affect comparisons between firms but also impair the validity of the asset figure for the industry as a whole. Naturally, the greater the period of time that separates the years for which the comparison is to be made the greater these difficulties of comparability are likely to be. As will be seen when the data of concentration in the U.K. and U.S.A. are presented below, value-added figures have in recent years been made available at fairly regular intervals in a reasonably convenient form for use in the study of concentration. But where the scope of the study extends back before the Second World War it has generally been necessary to make use of data relating also to employment and to assets.

Absolute concentration measures

There has been considerable controversy in the past over which concept of concentration and hence which form of measure is best suited to the purpose of indicating degrees of monopoly and competition in individual industries. Perhaps the most widely used measure to date has been the concentration ratio. The Census authorities, apart from giving a considerable body of information on such things as production, employment and sizes of plants and firms, also

give the proportion of each industry value added and employment accounted for by the largest enterprises. In the U.K.
the number is usually the three largest whereas in the U.S.A.
this information is given for the largest four, eight and twenty
enterprises.[1] This simple ratio of the proportion of total
industry output accounted for by the largest three or four
firms is termed the concentration ratio and has been used
extensively both in the U.K. and the U.S.A. The concentration
ratio is in effect derived from the industry concentration curve
which is plotted on a graph with horizontal scale marked off
from left to right in terms of the largest firms and the vertical
scale showing the cumulative percentage of industry output
(or other measure of size) produced by the *number* of firms
indicated on the horizontal scale. For illustrative purposes two
such curves are shown in Figure 1.

Since the vertical axis is measured off in terms of the cumulative share of a given number of the largest firms in the
industry, the concentration curve will rise throughout its
length from left to right. A steeply rising curve (e.g. chemicals
in Figure 1) which rapidly approaches the top of the vertical
scale indicates a highly concentrated industry, in which a
small number of firms share between them a large proportion
of the industry's output or assets. An industry of low concentration, on the other hand, will be indicated by a concentration curve whose slope rises only gently from left to
right (e.g. brewing in Figure 1). The number of firms shown
on the horizontal axis below the point where the slope of the
concentration curve flattens out indicates the 'focal point'
of concentration in the industry (see Blair, 1956, p. 359).
Although measuring the magnitude on the vertical scale in
terms of cumulative percentages means that no information is
contained in the diagram to indicate the relative importance
in the economy or in manufacturing industry of the industry
concerned, employing a scale of this kind does mean that

1. The Census authorities are bound to avoid disclosure of the
identity of individual firms and therefore in some cases the ratio may
refer in the U.K. to the largest four or more firms and in the U.S.A. to
the largest five or more.

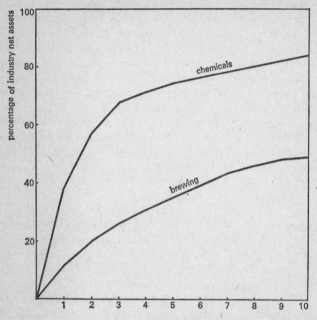

Figure 1 Concentration curves for quoted companies in the brewing and chemical industries, U.K., 1960, calculated from *Company Assets* (1962)

concentration curves for different industries are directly comparable. It is also evident from the diagram that the concentration *ratio* described above is simply one point on the concentration curve. Typically in the British Census of Production, for example, the information given corresponds to the point on the concentration curve above the three-firm mark on the horizontal axis.

Despite the simplicity of the concentration curve it has been used only rarely in the study of industrial concentration.[1] A major reason for this has probably been the lack of suffi-

1. An exception was Federal Trade Commission (1947), *The Concentration of Productive Facilities*.

cient information given in the Census of Production or Manufactures. It is evident from Figure 1 that to draw a concentration curve it is necessary to have output or asset data for the leading firms individually. But it has already been mentioned that the disclosure rules of the Census Authorities prevent them from giving such information. (The data used in Figures 1 and 2 were not taken from the Census of Production and relate only to *quoted* companies.)

A general criticism of the concentration curve is that it cannot be used to give a summary measure of the concentration level in the industry concerned. It would not be clear, for example, which of the following two industries is the more highly concentrated: industry A where two firms account for 50 per cent of the output and four firms account for 60 per cent; and industry B where two firms account for 40 per cent while four firms account for 75 per cent of output. In a diagram such as Figure 1 this difficulty would be indicated by the crossing of the two concentration curves. Since, as we have seen, the concentration ratio corresponds to one point only on the concentration curve there may be many changes in the position of the *curve* that leave the value of the *ratio* unchanged. In other words the ratio is not a summary measure based on the entire size distribution of firms in the industry nor does it even give the relative sizes of the largest three firms. Two industries, for example, may both have three-firm output concentration ratios of 80 per cent but in one case the largest firm may control 70 per cent of the total while in the other the largest firm may only account for 30 per cent of the total. Evidently, quite different market behaviour might be expected in the second industry compared with the first, particularly if in addition to the different relative sizes of the largest three firms, the remaining 20 per cent of output was shared in the second industry between only four firms while in the first industry another thirty firms were active. The dominance of the one firm in the first industry would probably lead to a stable pattern of monopolistic price or output control, with little threat to its position coming from other existing producers. In the second case, where the industry is a concentrated oligopoly, one of several patterns of behaviour is likely and it may change fundamentally from time to time. Periods of tacit collusion, for example, might be interrupted by price or product competition as possibly, one of the smaller firms attempts to gain a larger share of the market.

This limitation has led various writers to suggest concentration coefficients which give fuller information about the size distribution of firms in an industry. Fellner, for example, has suggested a three-number index composed of the share of the largest firm, the number of firms with shares exceeding, say, 10 per cent, and the joint share of the firms with shares exceeding 10 per cent (see National Bureau of Economic Research, 1955, p. 115). Although information in such detail is not yet available for a wide range of industries, from sources such as the Census of Production it is possible to build up a fairly detailed picture of the size structure of individual industries based on the concentration ratio and other indicators of size inequality. One recent study gives examples of different kinds of oligopolistic structure using information on the proportion of output or capacity accounted for by the largest four, eight and twenty firms together with the proportion supplied by all other firms (Bain, 1968, pp. 137–43). In chapter 6 below a detailed classification of market structures in the U.K. is made using the data prepared by Evely and Little (1960).

Inequality measures and concentration

The second kind of measure that has frequently been used in the study of industrial concentration is again best illustrated by means of a diagram. The vertical axis remains the same as in Figure 1, showing the cumulative percentages of a relevant economic measure of size, such as output or assets. On the horizontal axis is now shown the cumulative *percentage* of firms in the industry from the smallest to the largest. (In contrast, the concentration curve in Figure 1 showed on its horizontal axis the cumulative *number* of firms in the industry starting with the largest firm.) A Lorenz curve can then be formed by connecting up the points which indicate the cumulative percentage of output or assets accounted for by the various *percentages* of firms in the industry. Two examples of a Lorenz curve are shown in Figure 2. In an industry where all firms are of equal size the Lorenz curve would coincide with the diagonal which passes through the points 0,0 and 100,100 in Figure 2. Thus this line represents an industry where X per cent of firms account for X per cent of industry output or sales and it is commonly referred to as the line of equal distribution. Usually, of course, the largest X per cent of firms account for much more than X per cent of the industry output or sales. The further the Lorenz curve is from the line of equal distribution, the greater is the concentration of firms in the industry. Thus in Figure 2, for example, the

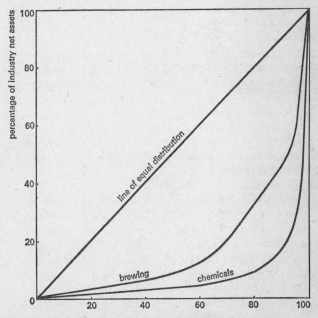

percentage of firms cumulated from the smallest sized firm

Figure 2 Lorenz curves for quoted companies in the brewing and chemical industries, U.K., 1960, calculated from *Company Assets* (1962)

chemical industry showed greater concentration in 1960 than the brewing industry.

It is possible to summarize the information shown by a Lorenz curve by means of the Gini coefficient which measures the area between the line of equal distribution and the Lorenz curve.[1] In other words, this concentration coefficient is a measure of the extent to which firms in the industry are unequal in size. For this reason it is common to refer to the Gini coefficient as a measure of *inequality* rather than of concentration. Since both the Lorenz curve and the Gini coefficient are based on the entire distribution of firms, changes at any point in the distribution, rather than simply a change amongst the largest firms, will be reflected in both of these measures. In an industry, for example, where a number of mergers take place between firms in the middle- and lower-size classes, there will be no change in the proportion of output or assets held by the largest three or four firms, i.e. the concentration *ratio* would remain unchanged. A change of this kind in the structure of the industry would, however, be reflected both in the Lorenz curve and the Gini coefficient. In the example mentioned the reduction in the number of firms in the industry, together with the reduced inequality in the sizes of the remaining firms following the mergers, may well lead to a *lower* value for the Gini coefficient corresponding to a Lorenz curve which has shifted inwards nearer to the diagonal of equal distribution.

In fact this example has also introduced one of the characteristics of the 'inequality' type of measure which has caused the controversy already mentioned. Since the Lorenz curve may well be affected by the *number* of firms in the industry it has been suggested that many of the changes that it may record in the size distribution are irrelevant from the point of view of a study of market structure. It is argued that in industries containing a multitude of small firms which in total account for a minute proportion of all industry output, a sudden

1. Various methods are available for the calculation of the Gini coefficient and there is a useful discussion of them in Singer (1968, pp. 144–9).

change in economic climate such as a recession may prove fatal for many of them with a consequent effect on the inequality measure. The effect on the market behaviour of the largest producers, however, is likely to be negligible since their relative position has remained unchanged.

A more practical difficulty has meant that measures of inequality like the Gini coefficient have been used less frequently in concentration studies than the concentration ratio. Data on the individual sizes and number of firms in the medium and small categories which are a necessary ingredient of an inequality measure are only rarely available, whereas the total industry size (measured in value added or employment) together with the proportion contributed by the largest firms is now readily available through the Census of Production or Manufactures.

The fundamental point of controversy has been concerned with which concept of concentration is more relevant to the study of market structure and for drawing inferences about industry behaviour. Those supporting the concentration ratio kind of measure have stressed the importance of the 'fewness' of sellers in an industry for this purpose. Those proposing 'inequality' type measures, while acknowledging their inappropriateness in cases where the number of sellers in an industry is very small, contend that the complete structure of an industry cannot be described without knowledge of all firms in the industry and that this kind of summary measure will have special advantages when the structure of industries are to be compared over time or between countries.

The search for a summary measure which could be used extensively in comparing concentration differences over time and between countries has led more recently to an exploration of the possibilities of finding a probability distribution that closely approximates the observed distribution of firms' sizes. So far some promising results have been achieved by using the 'lognormal' distribution. It is evident that the size distribution of firms measured in absolute terms is fairly heavily 'skewed' (i.e. a small number of firms usually accounts for a large proportion of total industry output or employment), and this precludes the direct application of the normal distribution and its familiar tests of significance in the study of firm size distributions. However, there is a good indication that when the *logarithms* of firms' sizes are taken in place of their absolute size, the resulting distribution does follow the 'normal' form fairly closely: hence the term 'lognormal' distribution. If it can be established that the distribution of the logarithms of firm sizes is normal then it is possible to use the variance of the logarithms as a summary measure of inequality (similar to the Gini coefficient), just as it is customary to use the variance of any distribution as a measure of inequality or dispersion. There is also the added advantage that the classical tests of significance can be applied to any estimate of size inequality.[1]

Thus efforts to find a unique measure which adequately describes the very complex subject of market structure have suggested two lines of approach: the concentration ratio or a measure of absolute concentration and the Gini coefficient and logarithmic variance as measures of inequality or relative concentration.

It should be remembered that the body of received theoretical analysis, particularly that relating to oligopoly, is not at all definite and clear cut in its predictions of market behaviour. Considering the number of different kinds of market structure that can be defined (see Bain, 1968, pp. 31–2), it would be surprising if a single numerical coefficient could provide anything more than a partial and preliminary indicator of all structural aspects of an industry relevant for classifying and comparing monopoly, oligopoly and competition. At present most information can probably be derived from a carefully combined use of both types of measure, recognizing at the same time that for a full judgement on the nature of competition to be made additional information is necessary on such factors as the rate of technological change, the degree of product differentiation and the rate of growth of demand.

1. A most influential article using this approach to the study of concentration is Hart and Prais (1956). See also Silberman, (1967).

4 Overall Concentration

The Significance of Large Absolute Size

Studies of overall concentration have attempted to estimate the proportion of all industrial activity in the economy as whole or in a broad sector of the economy, such as manufacturing, which is controlled by a small number or proportion of very large firms. They have typically examined the largest 100 or 200 enterprises, or those having more than, say, 5000 employees. The focus of attention is thus absolute size *per se* rather than relative size in a particular market. It has already been mentioned that there need not be any direct connexion between the two notions of absolute and relative size where, for example, a very large firm operates in several equally large markets. Where it can be established, however, that a high degree of overall concentration exists in a broad industrial sector, it is also likely that some individual markets will be highly concentrated.

Several lines of argument have been adopted to stress the significance of overall concentration. On a general political level it has been suggested that a large proportion of assets in private industry under the control of a relatively few firms can pose a threat to democratic government if some of those resources are used to influence political decisions through direct pressure group activity and, more indirectly, through advertising. Concern is also expressed about the inevitable bureaucracy which accompanies very large size, since this may mean that the number of individuals closely involved in making basic policy decisions on, for example, future investment, price and product policies – functions traditionally associated with entrepreneurship – becomes very small. Men in the middle and lower ranks of the executive hierarchy tend to be concerned more and more with routine and institutionalized decisions which allow little scope for initiative and which may in the long run affect the dynamism of the economy.

On the other hand it is often argued that a high level of overall concentration shown by a small number of firms *owning* a large proportion of economic resources may actually disguise an even greater degree of concentration of *control*. For within a company of large absolute size the control may rest in fact with one or two members of the board of directors, whose total ordinary shareholding may be very small in relation to the total ordinary capital of the company, but be large enough in relation to that of the other directors to give them a controlling influence. If in addition these same men are also directors of other large companies then total resources over which they have some influence may be doubly great. Considerable light was shed on these and related questions in a recent study covering a wide range of sizes of British industrial and commercial companies (see Florence, 1961). In practice it was found that ownership and control patterns were very complex and varied. For example, although one-third of the largest companies was identified as 'owner-controlled', it was also generally true that the divorce of ownership from control was more widespread amongst companies in this size group than those in smaller categories. This was reflected in three ways: a smaller average proportion of ordinary shares was owned by the board of directors; a smaller proportion of the companies had directors amongst their twenty largest ordinary shareholders; and more of the companies had directors whose shareholding was the minimum necessary to qualify them for a place on the board. Furthermore, within the boards of the largest companies there was considerable inequality in the shareholdings, which can probably be taken to reflect the internal balance of power. The average size of the boards of these companies was nine and on average between one and two directors were amongst the largest twenty shareholders, while at the same time between two and three held on average no more than the simple qualifying number of shares. On the question of the numbers of companies who had directors in common it was found that in almost one-half of the largest companies there was no overlap at all, although in just over one-fifth between three and five of the directors held similar positions in other companies. Without knowing the extent of the influence in each company of directors who hold several appointments it is not possible to say how far interconnexions of this kind actually increase the concentration of *control* over economic resources in a few hands. However, it is necessary to bear in mind these general characteristics of ownership and control when the data on overall concentration are considered below. Since for the most part these data relate to the amount of assets owned or output produced by companies, they do not take account of the relative positions of control actually exercised by individuals within companies. To the extent that control over major policy decisions *within* very large companies is itself concentrated, the degrees of overall concentration discussed below will tend to understate the actual position.

Another feature of large absolute size which has received increasing attention in recent years is the special economic power which a large diversified firm may be able to wield. On the assumption that diversification goes with large size, the important characteristic of such a firm is not so much that its output may have no raw materials, production process or ultimate function in common, but that it operates 'in a series of different markets, in each of which it encounters different competitors and different conditions of demand and supply' (Edwards, 1964, p. 38). Its activities are thus not confined to the boundaries of one market, and although its advantages derive from its large absolute size they are not those enjoyed by the monopolist, since the firm may not supply a large proportion of the output in any market in which it operates. It may suit the purposes of a diversified firm which has its resources spread throughout many different activities to subsidize products in some lines or in some areas if the market is geographically segmented, as part of a policy of long-run profit maximization regardless of short-run loss. The negative return on these lines can be covered by profits in other lines which may be facing less active competition. A policy of this kind may be very damaging to more specialized firms dependent for their overall profitability on those products which the diversified firm is subsidizing. The mere knowledge of the ability of a large diversified firm to engage for a considerable time in selective price cutting may be sufficient to ensure that specialized firms take no independent action as far as price changes are concerned.

Although the large diversified firm may use the subsidy as a long-run competitive instrument, it seems equally likely that the very complexity of its activities may make it prone to subsidize unintentionally. Even if the management's goal is to maximize profits in the short run as well as the long run this may not easily be achieved. Unless very detailed records are kept of the costs, prices and profits for every product it may be impossible to determine accurately which lines make profits and which make losses. The problem is made more difficult the larger the sum of overhead costs that have to be allocated between the firm's various activities. Some differences in profit margins are regarded as normal in very large firms and it seems likely in these circumstances that the evidence will have to be persistent and overwhelming before a company will decide to drop an unprofitable line. To the extent that true profits and losses remain camouflaged in this way the influence of the market as an allocative force on the economic resources of the diversified firm is neutralized.

There are two further ways in which the influence of large diversified firms may serve to deaden competition and lead to inefficient resource allocation. First, it is possible for such a firm to gain concessions from its specialist suppliers in the form of reciprocal purchases. The 'persuasive' powers of a large diversified firm on a smaller specialist producer, backed up by an implicit threat of sanctions if the latter does not agree, may well lead to a reciprocal buying arrangement between the two firms which in other circumstances the specialist firm might not have sought. Although the terms of the arrangement may not at first be any less favourable to the specialist firm than those it could have obtained elsewhere, there is the danger that changes in supply conditions will not lead to an adjustment of the agreement to the specialist firm's advantage, and furthermore, the reciprocal process might end with the specialist becoming merely a satellite supplier to the diversified firm. The general effect is to remove transactions between the specialist and the diversified firm from the bargaining of the market. To this extent competition is reduced.

Second, competition is likely to be reduced wherever diversified firms of similar overall size encounter each other in the market. The structure of such firms is likely to be such that while one has a stronger position in market A another is stronger in market B even though they both operate in each market. Under these circumstances it is unlikely to be in the interest of any large diversified firm to compete strongly in a market where it has an advantage and so risk retaliation in other markets where its position might not be so established.

In these ways the absolute size of large diversified firms can affect the market conduct and performance of an industry in which their relative market shares may not show the presence of monopoly or oligopoly.

We can now examine the available statistical data in order to decide whether a high level of overall concentration is present in the U.K. economy and also whether the assumption of large size accompanied by diversified output holds in practice.

The Level of Overall Concentration

Concentration amongst all concerns

Some preliminary idea of the degree of size inequality involved can be gained by considering Table 2, which shows the distribution of all concerns according to the size of their profits earned in 1961–2. The word 'concern' is used here in a very wide sense and includes not only private and public companies as described in the Companies Acts but also partnerships and individuals such as sole traders working for a profit.[1] An important omission from the table are the nationalized industries which are not assessed for profits tax and therefore are not included in the report from which Table 2 is taken.

Table 2
Size Distribution of All Concerns in the U.K., 1961–2, by Net True Income

Size (net true income)	Number (thousands)	Total amount (millions) (£ mill.)	Per cent of number	Per cent of net true income
Under 1000	1620·3	598·6	79·1	13·2
1000–9999	396·4	890·8	19·4	19·6
10,000–24,999	17·4	259·0	0·8	5·7
25,000–49,999	5·9	208·7	0·3	4·6
50,000–99,999	3·6	250·9	0·2	5·5
100,000–999,999	3·6	1005·7	0·2	22·1
1,000,000 and over	0·4	1336·9	0·02	29·4
Total	2047·6	4550·6	100·0	100·0

Source: Inland Revenue (1963), Table 42.

Although this is by no means an ideal set of data, it is sufficient for the following general observations about overall concentration to be made. Naturally since all sole traders and partnerships have been included as well as large public companies the total number of concerns is very large, well over two million, and the size differences are very great. But a large proportion of these concerns, 79 per cent, were very small and earned under £1000 profits in the year considered. In fact this group was responsible for only 13 per

1. Also included in the Inland Revenue Report from which Table 2 is taken are the commercial concerns of Local Authorities such as local transport undertakings, ports, etc. To this extent the figures include part of the publicly owned sector.

cent of total profits. If the two smallest size groups are taken together they amount to more than 98 per cent of the total number of concerns but earned only one-third of total profits. At the other end of the scale a minute fraction of the total number of concerns (approximately one-fifth of 1 per cent) earned more than half of total profits. These were the giant concerns earning profits of more than £1,000,000 per year.

Included so far in this general view of the industrial and commercial activity of the economy have been both financial and non-financial concerns. The former category includes such organizations as banks, insurance companies and hire purchase firms whose assets consist mainly of cash or securities issued by firms in the non-financial sector. In contrast, the assets of firms in the non-financial sector are for the most part plant, machinery and inventories of materials which are used in the production and distribution of goods and services. This sector includes, for example, agriculture, mining, manufacturing, distribution, construction and transport. A clearer picture of the concentration of control over *productive assets* in the economy would therefore emerge from a study of the non-financial sector alone. In fact this basic difference between the character of the assets held by the two sectors has led most students of the subject of industrial concentration to concern themselves almost exclusively with the non-financial sector.[1] The remainder of the present chapter, therefore, is concerned only with the non-financial sector of the economy.

Concentration in different industrial sectors

The available statistics allow a fairly detailed examination of overall concentration in different parts of the non-financial sector, in particular manufacturing, mining, quarrying and construction, retail distribution and agriculture. Together these industrial sectors accounted for 62 per cent of Gross Domestic Product in 1961.

1. One recent exception has been the discussion caused by the proposed mergers between three leading British banks, Lloyds, Barclays and Martins, and the subsequent report by the Monopolies Commission.

Information on the size distribution of firms in different sectors is presented in Table 3 and Table 4. Before discussing the light these tables throw on overall concentration it is important to stress several technical points which relate to the data used. The distributions are drawn from three separate sources and quite different measures of size are used. In Table 3, for example, size is measured in terms of numbers employed, whereas in Table 4, part A, it is number of establishments per organization and in part B it is number of acres. This is one reason why it is not possible to compare directly Table 3 and the two parts of Table 4. Second, the unit of classification of size also differs. In Table 2 this is the *enterprise* defined by the Census authorities as 'one or more firms under common ownership or control as defined by the Companies Act, 1948 ....' An enterprise normally consists either of a single firm or a holding company together with its subsidiary companies. The table also gives the number of separate establishments or plants owned by enterprises in the various groups. In Table 4, part A, the number of establishments is also given but here they are grouped by *organization* and not enterprise. The organization unit used in this context is not such a comprehensive controlling unit as the enterprise. For example, in the case of one enterprise which controlled two companies, one running a series of, say, grocery shops and the other a chain of shoe stores, this would be included as two organizations in Table 4, part A, although there is actually only one controlling enterprise.[1] For present purposes, therefore, the *organization* data in Table 4, part A, probably tends to understate the level of overall concentration in retailing. Fuller information on enterprise control might well show a greater proportion of turnover accounted for by firms in the larger size groups. Similarly in Table 4, part B, where the classifying unit is the agricultural holding, there is no consolidation to show the number of holdings and total acreage held by one company through its subsidiaries. This

1. Some information on control at the enterprise level is given in the 1961 Census of Distribution, part 14, but does not include small enterprises and was therefore not used in the context of this chapter.

Table 3
Enterprises by Employment Size, 1958

Size of enterprise by number of persons employed	Manufacturing industry				Mining, quarrying and construction			
	No. of enterprises	No. of establishments	% of total employment	% of total net output	No. of enterprises	No. of establishments	% of total employment	% of total net output
5000 and over	180	3788	34·3	38·3	5	9	4·1	5·5
1000–4999	777	4200	20·6	21·7	90	358	14·4	17·2
500–999	993	2808	9·2	8·6	138	309	7·3	8·6
100–499	7240	11,317	20·1	17·9	1420	1680	21·1	21·9
25–99	14,257	16,549	9·9	8·4	5207	5464	19·7	19·6
1–24	n.a.	47,297	5·9	5·2	n.a.	88,471	33·3	27·4

n.a.: not available

Source: Board of Trade (1962).

again is likely to be a source of some understatement of the actual level of overall concentration in the agricultural sector. Although the Census of Production data given in Table 3 are consolidated in the sense of showing the total number of separate plants legally owned by a parent company, in common with the information in Table 4, it cannot show the precise extent of *de facto* control exercised by one company over another in which it may have only a minority shareholding. It is certainly possible for such control to exist although the extent to which it occurs in practice is difficult to establish. However, when considering the data in Tables 3 and 4, it is necessary to bear this source of understatement in mind.

Despite these general limitations on the data they are adequate for the present purpose of indicating degrees of overall concentration in different industrial sectors. A high level of overall concentration will occur when a small proportion of the number of firms control a large proportion of the total output, employment, etc. A convenient benchmark for this purpose is the proportion of the total sector activity controlled by the largest 1 per cent of firms. This was used by Florence (1961, p. 8) in his study of large firms where he notes that the size distribution of all *firms* in the economy exhibits much greater inequality than both the size distribution of capital and income. If we are to employ this measure in connexion with Table 3, however, we need to know the total number of enterprises in the industries included. The Census authorities do not give a figure for the total number of enterprises in the smallest size class although they do give the total number of establishments in this size class.[1] From the first two columns of Table 3, it is evident that enterprises in the second smallest size class in manufacturing industry owned just over one establishment each on average. It is

1. It should also be noted that figures relating to the two smallest size classes are based on less complete information than that for enterprises having more than 100 employees. But the broad generalizations about overall size inequality are unlikely to be greatly affected by the estimates for the smallest size grouping.

likely, therefore, that in the smallest size class there was approximately only one establishment per enterprise. The number of establishments in this class gives an upper limit to the number of enterprises, while a lower limit can be estimated by assuming that there was a similar number of establishments per enterprise in the smallest size class as in the next smallest. This procedure can be adopted both for manufacturing industry and mining, quarrying and construction. In both cases the estimated number of enterprises in the smallest size class, whether the lower or upper limit is taken, is very large in relation to the numbers in the other size groups. In manufacturing industry just over 1 per cent of all enterprises account for about 60 per cent of total output and 55 per cent of total employment. All firms in this category employed over 1000 people in 1958 but it is also significant that there was a smaller group of 180 firms (representing approximately one-quarter of 1 per cent of the total) each having more than 5000 employees and accounting for more than a third of total manufacturing employment and 38 per cent of net output. In contrast, enterprises in the smallest size group are estimated to amount to more than 60 per cent of the total *number* but to account for only about 5 per cent of total output and employment.

This pattern of concentration is not repeated in the mining, quarrying and construction industries shown in the right hand part of Table 3. Using assumptions similar to those made above for manufacturing industry it is evident that an even greater preponderance of enterprises, over 90 per cent, appear in the smallest size classes. In contrast with manufacturing industry, however, the smallest firms account for a substantial amount of employment, 33 per cent, and net output, 27 per cent. In fact, firms in the *two* smallest size categories were responsible for about one-half the total employment and output in these industries in 1958. There were far fewer large and very large firms in these industries than in manufacturing and the ninety-five largest enterprises which employed more than 1000 people in 1958 accounted for about one-fifth of total employment and output. But the very great number of extremely small firms, most of which were probably in the construction industry, also means that the largest firms only formed a small fraction of 1 per cent of the total number. Thus although great disparity in sizes is apparent in both the sectors considered so far, the small number of very large firms play a much more important part in manufacturing industry.

In many respects the pattern of firm sizes in the retail trade is similar to that in the mining and construction group, with a great number of very small concerns responsible in total for a substantial proportion of the trade. This information is shown in the first part of Table 4. Practically all retail organizations owned between one and four establishments and accounted for almost 60 per cent of total retail turnover. On the other hand organizations with fifty or more establishments amounting to less than one-tenth of 1 per cent of the total number were responsible for about a quarter of total turnover. Again there is great inequality in size between the smallest and largest firms, and also in the aggregate the largest firms are relatively less dominant than in manufacturing. This conclusion would probably not be greatly altered if complete information were available on the extent to which separate enterprises actually controlled more than one organization, although it has already been pointed out (see above) that this is a possible source of understatement of overall control by large firms in the retail trade.

Finally in this section, we can consider the position in agriculture, traditionally regarded as a sector dominated by many relatively small independent farmers. The data presented in the right hand portion of Table 4 contain sources of understatement of the actual level of control similar to that for the retail trade. In comparison with the other sectors examined, there appears to be generally less inequality in size. On the one hand the proportion of all holdings in the smallest two categories is much less than in manufacturing, mining and retail distribution, but at the same time the small proportion of very large farms, 2 per cent of the total, are quantitatively much less significant than their counterparts in manufactur-

Table 4
Size Distribution of Organizations in Retailing, and Agricultural Holdings

A. Retail distribution, 1961				B. Agricultural holdings, 1964		
Organizations other than co-operative societies having:	No. of organizations	No. of establishments	% of turnover	Size of holding (acres)	% of all holdings	% of total acreage
100 establishments and over	140	37,916	21·7	500 & over	2·0	21·1
50–99	122	8277	3·7	150–499	14·4	42·7
20–49	350	10,351	5·5	50–149	24·8	26·4
10–19	688	9057	3·6	20–49	16·2	6·4
5–9	2971	18,279	6·0	5–19	22·2	2·7
2–4	31,809	76,016	13·5	under 5	20·4	0·7
1 establishment	316,362	316,362	46·0	—	—	—

Source: A—Board of Trade (1963).
B—Ministry of Agriculture (1967).

ing industry. A sizeable proportion of all farms, just on 40 per cent, are in the 50- to 500-acre range and account for 69 per cent of the total acreage. Thus agriculture appears to be neither dominated by a small number of very large concerns nor composed of a multitude of very small concerns which are quantitatively significant.

Companies and overall concentration

The information considered so far has included industrial activity carried on by all forms of organization: the public and private company, the partnership and the individual trader. It appears that overall concentration, interpreted as the share of the activity controlled by a small number or proportion of firms, is considerably more pronounced in manufacturing than in the other sectors examined. But it has often been stressed that for the purpose of estimating the extent to which industrial activity is concentrated in the hands of a few concerns it is only companies that really need to be considered. In connexion with his study of the largest companies in British industry Florence (1961) made a tentative estimate that out of nearly two million concerns (including financial enterprises) which were assessed for trading profit in 1951–2 by the Inland Revenue authorities, the 100 largest industrial and commercial companies accounted for 20 per cent of the aggregate profit of all trading concerns and the largest 1700 companies, having an income of £200,000 or more, were responsible for 40 per cent of all business done by private enterprise. In those sectors that we have examined in the previous section a more recent report (Inland Revenue, 1963, tables 43–60) shows that the company form of organization accounted for 96 per cent of profits in manufacturing and mining and quarrying; about 46 per cent in construction and retail distribution and only 9 per cent in agriculture. A remarkably similar pattern for these and the other industrial sectors has been quoted for the U.S. economy (see, for example Mason, ed., 1961, p. 87), suggesting that some fundamental factors are at work making the company a more suitable form of industrial organization in some sectors than in others. Not least of these are manufacturing industry's large capital requirements which can apparently be met only where the principles of corporate identity and limited liability are accompanied by highly organized capital markets.

It is possible to examine in more detail the company part of manufacturing industry which has so far appeared to have both a high level of overall concentration and also practically all of its profits earned by companies rather than by partnerships or individual traders.

Detailed information is available only for those companies in manufacturing which have shares quoted on the stock exchange. It thus excludes the considerable number of private companies which are unquoted and which are for the most part small, as well as some large unquoted subsidiaries of foreign firms. By limiting consideration to the quoted company part of manufacturing industry the number of enterprises is reduced from over 60,000 (in Table 3) to less than 1500. Yet although we are now examining only the larger end of all firms in manufacturing the degree of overall concentration *within* this group is still great. Thus at the end of 1963 the largest ninety-six firms, each having net assets of £25 million or more, controlled 65 per cent of aggregate net assets in manufacturing. Together they represented less than 7 per cent of the number of quoted companies covered. Naturally, these aggregate figures obscure considerable differences within different parts of manufacturing industry. Companies in this size category accounted for more than 80 per cent of net assets in chemicals, tobacco and metal manufacturing, but only between one-quarter and one-third in non-electrical engineering, shipbuilding and brick and pottery manufacture.

The extent to which this level of overall concentration in manufacturing has been increasing over time and also the concentration levels in individual markets are subjects for subsequent chapters. But we have still to decide whether it is generally true that large absolute size is accompanied by diversified output since, as was mentioned above, these two factors together can have important economic implications.

According to a recent study of diversification in British manufacturing industry based on the Census of Production for 1958 there was a clear increase in the extent of diversification the larger the enterprise (see Amey, 1964, p. 265). Diversification was gauged by the number of different industry groups in which an enterprise operated through its various establishments. Even though the smallest enterprises employing less than 100 people could not be included in the analysis, the difference in diversification between the four other size groups of enterprises was striking. For example, among enterprises in the largest size group each having more than 5000 employees, 37 per cent of the number producing 55 per cent of the group's net output operated in five or more industries. The most diversified 9 per cent of enterprises in this size group producing 21 per cent of its net output operated in ten or more separate industries. No firms in the other size groups approached this degree of diversification. The proportion of enterprises operating in five or more industries in the smallest size group was a negligible proportion of the group total and applied to only 5 per cent of the enterprises in the second largest size group (employing between 1000 and 5000 people). At the other extreme, whereas 91 per cent of enterprises in the smallest size group producing 89 per cent of its output operated in one industry, in the largest size group only 21 per cent, responsible for 11 per cent of the group net output, was so specialized.

Concern about the possible harmful effects that could flow from increased diversification by merger recently found expression in the Monopolies and Mergers Act, 1965, which provides for the Monopolies Commission, at the request of the Board of Trade, to investigate proposed mergers, not only where they may tend to increase monopoly but also simply where the value of assets to be acquired is in excess of £5 million. The increased proportion of mergers of this type in the U.S.A. often referred to as conglomerate has also aroused considerable interest. Amongst large firms, for example, the proportion of acquisitions classified as conglomerate has risen from about 59 per cent in the period 1948–53 to 71 per cent in the early 1960s (Mueller, 1964, p.516). The difficulties that these developments cause for anti-trust policy are discussed further in chapter 8.

5 Market Concentration

Introduction

As was mentioned at the beginning of chapter 1 above, one of the implications of the theories of imperfect and monopolistic competition which came to be emphasized by economists was that under certain conditions it was possible for the effects of monopoly to be prevalent even in the ostensible absence of monopolies as such. It was postulated that market 'imperfections' could indeed constitute the conditions from which monopolistic consequences might result. This theoretical implication has been the reason for the much greater interest shown in the study of levels of concentration in individual markets than in broad sectors of the economy. Coupled with the barriers to new competition and the degree of product differentiation, the number and size distribution of firms is recognized as being one of the structural features of the market which has an important bearing on the behaviour and performance of firms.

The predictions of economic theory about the two extremes of market structure, monopoly and perfect competition, are quite unequivocal and definite. The policy of the monopolist will simply be to adjust price or output in accordance with his underlying cost structure in order to maximize profit. Competition, except in the rather distant sense that ultimately all products compete with each other, is completely lacking. In contrast, firms in a competitive industry are so small in relation to the total that they have individually no influence over price which is determined by the twin influences of market demand and supply. Each adjusts his own output in order to maximize his profit at the market price.

In both cases the behaviour of the firms in regard to prices and output is a *function of the structure of the market*. Similarly, it is possible to go one stage further in the analysis to derive the familiar results reflecting the performance of monopolist and of the firms in a competitive industry. In long-run equilibrium, for example, the monopolist will probably not operate at the optimum output (minimum unit costs) and he will earn profits in excess of the opportunity cost of his capital. By comparison the continual adjustment process of the competitive industry will ensure that in equilibrium in the long run all firms will operate at minimum unit costs and also earn a return equivalent to the opportunity cost of capital.

To the extent that industries in real life appear to approximate in their structure to the competitive industry of economic theory, it is reasonable to expect that their behaviour and performance will likewise be reasonably competitive. Individual firms will have little or no control over the prices set and they will be obliged to seek efficient production methods or risk failure. It is also possible, although here the market situation is already becoming complex enough not to yield a simple answer, that a structure approximating monopoly will produce results similar to those predicted by the theory of monopoly. Where an industry is composed, for example, of a few large firms each one may well be prepared to give up some independence in setting prices or output level in order to ensure that profits for the group as a whole are maximized. In any case, an industrial structure of this type circumscribes to a considerable extent the freedom of action of individual sellers simply because a change in the price policy of one will have a distinct and immediate effect on the returns of the others. Once we depart slightly from the extreme market structure of monopoly, the industry becomes oligopolistic with the central feature of interdependence between sellers. No one firm can make a change in any of its major policy variables without causing a reaction amongst its competitors. It is clear in an industry of five firms each having an equal market share that any attempt by one firm to improve its own position by 10 per cent will produce retaliatory action, since each will know not only which firm has attempted to upset the *status quo* but also that it stands to lose more than 5 per cent of its own market share. In the empirical classification of market structures, however, the difficulty arises of deciding exactly where such complete interdependence is likely to stop and give way to behaviour more closely linked with a competitive industry. It is not clear, for example, that in an industry composed of, say, ten firms each holding a roughly equal share of the market, that all will behave as though any individual action will produce a counter-measure from the other firms. For in this case the attempt by one firm to increase its market share by 10 per cent is only likely to affect its competitors to the extent of just over 1 per cent of their sales. It may also be difficult to determine exactly which firm had initiated the change. The market situation may be further complicated as the number of firms becomes larger by some inequality in their size distribution. Several large firms may account for a substantial fraction of total industry output but the presence of a large number of small firms each having perhaps 1 per cent or less of the market may affect the character of competition in the industry even though the large firms see no immediate threat to their own position from the action of the smaller sellers. The presence of a fringe of small sellers, may, for example, tend to keep the price levels, established by the joint action of the large firms, at a level lower than would have prevailed in their absence.

Thus although theory highlights the essential features of an oligopolistic market structure – a relatively small number of large firms aware of their interdependence – it does not delineate the actual number of firms which in practice will produce a particular pattern of oligopoly behaviour. As a consequence, most empirical studies of industrial concentration which seek to identify those industries most likely to be competitive and those most likely to be oligopolistic have had to use their own judgement as to the *level of concentration that forms the dividing point*. For example, in the most detailed study of concentration in British industry, which will be referred to frequently in the present and next chapters, Evely and Little made the initial threefold distinction between industries of high concentration where the largest three firms account for 67 per cent or more of total output or employment; industries of medium concentration where the largest three firms account for between 34 and 66 per cent of output or employment, and industries of low concentration in which the largest three firms account for up to 33 per cent of output or employment (Evely and Little, 1960, p. 51).

The concentration ratio by itself gives a useful preliminary idea of the type of market structures in existence and those industries where oligopolistic or competitive behaviour is likely. Thus an industry with a concentration ratio of under 10 per cent is likely to exhibit patterns of behaviour approximating a competitive industry. This kind of behaviour would be precluded in an industry with a concentration ratio as high as, say, 80 per cent. Generally, however, if a detailed classification of market structure is to be attempted, the concentration ratio has to be supplemented by further information about the relative sizes of the other firms in the industry. One method widely adopted in the U.S.A. is to use the four- or eight-firm concentration ratio with information on the proportion of output also supplied by the largest twenty and fifty firms, together possibly with the total number of firms in the industry. One well known study, for example, distinguishes between concentrated and unconcentrated industries. Concentrated industries are further divided into type 1 oligopolies where the first eight firms make 50 per cent or more of total sales and the first twenty make 75 per cent or more; and type 2 oligopolies where the first eight firms make 33 per cent or more of total sales and the first twenty make less than 75 per cent. An industry is classified as unconcentrated in this scheme if the first eight firms make less than 33 per cent of total sales (Kaysen and Turner, 1959, p. 27). The distinction was made between the two types of oligopoly in an attempt in the first case to isolate those industries where the few biggest sellers have market shares large enough to recognize their mutual dependence, while in the second case the distinguishing feature was the existence of the relatively unconcentrated sector which could have a varying influence on the behaviour of the largest firms.

The data available to Evely and Little in their study did not allow a similar extension of the concentration ratio concept but they did attempt to classify industries in a detailed fashion by the use of the *size-ratio of units* (or firms). This 'measures the average size of the three largest units relative to the average size of other units in the trade' (Evely and Little, 1960, p. 38). Consequently in an industry where the three-firm concentration ratio is 75 per cent but where there are only five firms altogether, the size ratio of units would be: the average size of the largest three firms (25 per cent of the total) divided by the average size of the other remaining firms (12·5 per cent), i.e. two. Alternatively, a much higher size ratio of units reflects a larger disparity in size amongst firms in the industry. For example, in another industry with a 75 per cent three-firm concentration ratio, if the total number of firms was twenty-five this means that the twenty-two smaller firms account for one-quarter of total output and the size ratio of units is twenty-two. As we shall see below the combination of the concentration ratio and the size ratio allows a much more satisfactory analysis of market structures having different levels of concentration.

Concentration in Private Industry

This section draws heavily on the results of the Evely and Little study into the level of concentration in British manufacturing industry in 1951. It is as well at the outset to comment briefly on the coverage and method of the study. Although the study was published in 1960 much of it related to the year 1951. Since that time more information has been published for 1958 in the Census of Production and similar material may be shortly available for 1963.[1] In the next chapter some reference

1. At the time of writing, the 1963 Census of Production had been published only in part.

will be made to the changes in concentration that took place between 1951 and 1958. For the most part these changes have not been profound, and in any case the comprehensiveness and depth of the Evely and Little study make it an unrivalled source on industrial concentration in the U.K. The data analysed in the first three parts of the study were drawn basically from the Census of Production for 1951, supplemented in part three by similar material for 1935. For the year 1951 the published information was considerably enriched by additional data specially prepared for the study by the Board of Trade. The 147 trades (which for present purposes can be regarded as synonymous with industries) of the Census were subdivided to yield information on 200 of the constituent sub-trades. Where the sub-trade approached more closely the industry concept of economic theory it was used in preference to the wider trade. The industries or trades covered in the study included extractive, manufacturing and processing industries, together with a few service trades and represented 'the bulk of privately owned industry in the United Kingdom' (Evely and Little, 1960, p. 49).

In order to obtain the most economically meaningful results on market structure a considerable pruning of the total population of industries was made. In particular all industries with levels of specialization and exclusiveness[1] below 67 per cent were left out of the subsequent analysis. Some other industries were omitted because of inadequate or unsatisfactory data and this selection process left a total of 220 industries which had a total employment of just under $6\frac{1}{2}$ million, representing about 63 per cent of the total industrial employment covered by the Census of Production in 1951.

Grouping industries in the sample according to whether concentration was high, medium or low yielded the following results:

1. The interpretation of these terms in relation to Census industries was explained in chapter 3.

Table 5
Distribution of 220 Trades by Concentration Category, 1951

Concentration category (employment or net output)	Trades		Employment	
	number	percentage of total	thousands	percentage of total
High (67 per cent and over)	50	23	636	10
Medium (34–66 per cent)	69	31	1545	24
Low (33 per cent and under)	101	46	4188	66
Total	220	100	6369	100

Source: Evely and Little, 1960, p. 51.

It may be somewhat surprising that practically two-thirds of total sample employment was in industries of low concentration in 1951, while only 10 per cent was in high concentration industries. If the concentration ratio alone could be taken as an adequate description of industrial structure, then Table 5 would appear to suggest that only a small fraction of British industry was likely to show monopolistic behaviour and performance. As pointed out above, however, before any such judgement can be made a more detailed description of the size distribution of firms associated with the level of concentration is necessary.

The importance of different levels of concentration will also vary according to the size of the industry in relation to the economy and, more important, according to its position in the economic process. The organization of investment goods industries is likely to be more important from the point of view of resource allocation than consumer goods industries. This is because producers' goods will not only affect the prices of subsequent goods which they help to make but also production processes and product designs. Thus a monopolistically high price for steel may well cause users of steel to change their product design (in favour, say, of aluminium) in order to minimize its use. The ultimate result may be a widespread change in the level of efficiency amongst manufacturing industries, whereas monopoly in consumer goods industries will have the less important result of higher prices to consumers with a consequent transfer of income from consumers to producers.

Evely and Little did not make a separate classification of industries according to broad type of industrial activity but it is evident from their tables (Evely and Little, 1960, pp. 51–60, Tables 2, 3 and 4), that within each concentration group there is a considerable variety of industries as well as large variations in the size of industries and the number of firms per industry. Thus no simple patterns emerged to indicate that, for example, industries of high concentration were also generally producer goods industries and contained only a few firms.

One way of summarizing the concentration data for the 220 industries in order to give an approximate idea of which broad areas of industry are more heavily concentrated is presented in Table 6 which gives employment and net output concentration for sixteen broad industrial categories. The concentration figures given were obtained by weighting the employment (or net output) concentration ratio for each industry by the industry's employment (or net output). Although too much weight should not be placed on the concentration ratios obtained in this way they are useful for highlighting those areas of industry where concentration levels are greatest.

Naturally the average concentration ratios for each industry group embodies a whole range of concentration ratios for individual industries. Generally speaking, those sectors of industry associated with very large capital requirements appear amongst the most heavily concentrated, such as chemicals and allied trades, electrical engineering and electrical goods, vehicles and iron and steel and non-ferrous metals. On the other hand, sectors usually associated with smaller firms tended to rank low in terms of concentration, e.g. cotton, woollen and worsted, clothing and footwear, and building and contracting.

Within the broad limitations of Census data a much fuller description of market structures can be made by using the concentration ratio in conjunction with the size distribution of firms. For analysing industrial structure in 1951, Evely and Little used the category of concentration (determined by the three firm concentration ratio), the size-ratio of firms, and the number of firms in the industry. The use of these additional structural characteristics allows interesting distinctions to be made between industries with the same level of concentration but quite different overall structure. Industries of medium concentration, for example, fell into three distinct categories:

Table 6

Concentration of Employment and Net Output by Industry Groups, 1951

Broad industrial category	Number of industries	Average level of concentration	
		Employment (%)	Net output (%)
Chemicals and allied trades	16	51	46
Electrical engineering and electrical goods	8	48	46
Vehicles	8	41	44
Iron and steel and non-ferrous metals	15	39	40
Drink and tobacco	7	36	42
Mining and quarrying and mining products	21	35	41
Shipbuilding and non-electrical engineering	20	31	32
Food	18	30	35
Other metal industries	27	29	32
Other textiles	18	27	36

Broad industrial category	Number of industries	Average level of concentration	
		Employment (%)	Net output (%)
Paper and printing	10	21	24
Cotton	3	21	18
Other manufacturing and service trades	23	20	23
Woollen and worsted	6	18	18
Clothing and footwear	17	14	12
Building, contracting and civil engineering	3	12	11
Total	220	29	33

Source: Evely and Little (1960), p. 62.

those with many firms and large size-ratios (indicating a considerable size difference between the largest three firms and the remainder); those with few firms and small size-ratios; and those with many firms and small size-ratios. Now although all of these industries had concentration ratios between 34–66 per cent it seems unlikely that they would all have similar behaviour. Industries with few firms and small size-ratios are likely to be characterized by tacit or overt collusion amongst the leading firms who may jointly be able to exercise considerable monopoly power even though concentration is not extreme. In contrast, those industries with many firms and small size ratios may exhibit strong competitive features, modified if the largest firms who control at least one-third of the industry can organize an agreement amongst themselves to increase their control. Similar distinctions within the other concentration categories were made by Evely and Little and they also suggested the kind of behaviour that could be expected to flow from the different market structures.

An attempt has been made to summarize all of this

information in Table 7 below where three main structural groups are considered. Group 1 brings together industries where the concentration level and industrial structure are most likely to produce monopoly power exercised by one dominant firm or a dominant group acting together. The three kinds of highly concentrated industries distinguished by Evely and Little are all included within Group 1 together with two further kinds having only medium concentration. The reason why these industries of medium concentration are classified in Group 1 as likely to exhibit behaviour similar to that associated with concentrated oligopoly lies in their overall structure. Thus even though concentration is only medium, when there are many firms and also a large size-ratio the largest firms are likely to be able to exert considerable influence over the industry as a whole. In particular, they may be able to ensure through joint action that none of their smaller rivals can grow sufficiently to threaten their own position.

The central characteristic of industries in Group 2 is the association of a large number of firms with either a medium level of concentration and small size-ratios or low concentration and a large size-ratio. In both cases the presence of some firms large in relation to the industry precludes behaviour like that expected in a competitive industry. Furthermore, in many of those industries with low concentration and a large size-ratio Evely and Little show that the average size of the largest firms is great in an absolute sense as well as in relation to the industry and suggest that in these cases such firms will probably be price leaders with considerable market power *vis-à-vis* their smaller rivals. Nevertheless, the presence of a large number of smaller firms may, in these industries where the concentration ratio is not high, have the effect of modifying the pricing policies of the largest firms. In order, for example, to contain the smaller firms the industry leaders may set prices below those representing joint profit maximization. But the probable scale and marketing advantages possessed by the larger firms will effectively prevent prices being reduced to the competitive level.

Only in those industries in Group 3 where a low concentra-

Table 7
Market Structures in the U.K., 1951

Main group	Structural characteristics				Number of industries	% of sample employment
		Concentration category	Number of firms	Size ratio of firms		
Group 1 (Monopoly and concentrated oligopoly)		1. High	Few	Large	20	3
		2. High	Many	Large	13	4
		3. Medium	Many	Large	25	18
		4. High	Few	Small	17	3
		5. Medium	Few	Small	15	2
Group total					90	30
Group 2 (Unconcentrated oligopoly)		6. Medium	Many	Small	29	6
		7. Low	Many	Large	40	43
Group total					69	49
Group 3 (Competitive)		8. Low	Many	Small	60	21
Grand total					219	100

Source: Compiled from Evely and Little, 1960, chapter 5.

tion ratio is associated with a large number of firms and a small firm size ratio is it likely that market behaviour and performance will approach that predicted for a competitive industry. The sixty industries in Group 3 of Table 7 only accounted for 21 per cent of the total employment in industries covered by the Evely and Little sample, although it was seen in Table 5 above that almost two-thirds of total employment was in industries of low concentration. Similarly those industries where monopolistic or concentrated oligopoly behaviour is thought most likely, account for 30 per cent of total employment in Table 7 yet only 10 per cent of total employment was in industries of high concentration.

Thus the more detailed analysis of concentration *with* overall industry structure indicates the far wider existence of possible oligopolistic influences than is given by the concentration ratio alone. A similar conclusion was reached by Kaysen and Turner in their analysis of market structures in U.S. manufacturing industry in 1954 (Kaysen and Turner, 1959, chapter 2). Although they do not use exactly the same criteria for dividing industries into different broad groups (see above) the central characteristics of market structure that they attempt to isolate in their three main groups are broadly similar to those set out in Table 7 for U.K. industry. For all manufacturing industries in their analysis they found that the concentrated oligopoly of type 1 accounted for 22 per cent of the total sales of the industries covered. The less concentrated oligopoly of type 2 accounted for 40 per cent of sales, and the remaining 38 per cent were made by industries of a competitive type. The data used are not closely comparable because of the differences in definition and measurement, but they do permit the following two broad generalizations. In both countries the greater part of (mainly) manufacturing industries have some definite elements of oligopoly or monopoly, although the most heavily concentrated sectors only accounted for 22–30 per cent of the total. It also seems possible that the unconcentrated, competitive sector is considerably more important in U.S. industry than in the U.K.

Several investigations have attempted to compare directly

levels of concentration in the U.K. and U.S.A. based simply on the concentration ratio. There are formidable problems in making a satisfactory international comparison of this kind, mostly arising from the different definitions and coverage of the basic data. It is quite common, for example, for separate industries to be defined differently in the two countries, making an exact comparison impossible. Also, if industries are defined generally on a broader basis in one country than another this will probably give lower concentration ratios and tend to yield misleading results in any comparison. In the U.S. Census of Manufactures a concentration ratio for the largest *four* firms is given whereas in the U.K. Census of Production the ratio refers to the largest *three* firms and therefore some adjustment is necessary before any comparison can be made.

One study relating to the year 1935 concluded that the general level of concentration in British industries was higher than in their American counterparts (see Rosenbluth, 1955, pp. 70–77). An overall comparison was made initially without having to reconcile individual industry classifications. The method was to construct a frequency distribution of industries at 10 per cent intervals according to their level of concentration. The percentage of industries and employment having concentration ratios above any specified level was consistently higher in the U.K. than the U.S.A. For example, whereas 28 per cent of British industries accounting for 19 per cent of employment had concentration ratios of 50 per cent or more, the comparable figures for American industries were 22 per cent and 14 per cent. The weighted average concentration index worked out at 33 per cent for the U.K. and 19 per cent for the U.S.A. Amongst fifty-seven industries that could be matched sufficiently well to make a reasonable comparison possible, thirty-three had higher concentration in the U.K. than in the U.S.A., while in twenty-four concentration was higher in the U.S.A. But the average difference in the concentration indexes was greater in the former industries than in the latter.

Little support, however, is given to the broad conclusion

that U.K. industry is more highly concentrated than that in the U.S.A. by two further studies which relate basically to the year 1951 (Shepherd, 1961, pp. 70–75, and Bain, 1966, pp. 76–81). Both investigations concluded that there appeared to be little difference between concentration levels in the two countries, with if anything the possibility that it was marginally higher in the U.S.A. than in the U.K. Bain, for example, examined thirty-two industries which could be directly compared and found that in nine cases concentration was approximately the same in both countries, in twelve it was lower in the U.K. and in eleven higher in the U.K., than in the U.S.A. But in this study greater divergences in concentration between the two countries were found on average between industries where the U.K. had *lower* concentration. There is the possibility, of course, that concentration in the U.K. actually declined over the period 1935–51 while remaining stable or slightly increasing in the U.S.A., and this proposition is examined in more detail in the next chapter. In general, however, the available evidence is far from conclusive that concentration is higher in the U.K. This is despite factors, for example, like the smaller U.K. market which might only allow the presence of a relatively few firms of optimum scale and the weaker and more recent anti-trust policy, both of which would indicate higher concentration levels in the U.K.

6 Changes in Concentration over Time

Introduction

The review in the two previous chapters of concentration data relating to the 1950s and early 1960s has suggested that in important sectors and markets of the U.K. and U.S.A. economies the levels of concentration are high. This conclusion immediately prompts the question of whether the level of concentration has always been the same or whether there has been some persistent upward or downward trend. If the latter, then it would also be very interesting to know whether the trend is likely to continue into the future, and an answer to this question can only be given once the forces underlying any discernible trend have been analysed and understood. The importance of these questions took on a special significance in the 1930s when it was widely suggested that the prognoses of Marx and his followers concerning the breakdown of capitalism following a continued increase in industrial concentration had been proved correct.

As far as the available statistical data allow, this chapter attempts to determine whether there has been a general trend in concentration levels and it is convenient for this purpose to maintain the distinction between overall and market concentration that has hitherto been followed.

The Trend in Overall Concentration

In addition to the special data problems which are associated with most economic time series where the period to be considered is necessarily longer than about twenty years, other difficulties of interpretation are encountered in the study of changes in industrial concentration. It is very important, for example, to realize that the decline in significance in the economy of a relatively unconcentrated sector while in all other sectors concentration levels remain unchanged will mean that overall concentration for the economy as a whole will have increased. Where concentration is thought of in terms of the share of assets, output or national income, etc., accounted for by the largest enterprises, then the process of industrialization in itself will bring about an increase in overall concentration. For this process involves a large increase in the manufacturing and public utility sectors where the typical enterprise is relatively large, and a comparable decline in the importance of agriculture where the typical enterprise is relatively small. This leads one authority on American industrial organization to conclude that 'the most important explanation of changes in general concentration lies in shifts in economic activity among sectors with different degrees of concentration, rather than in changes in the degree of concentration in these sectors' (Mason, 1957, p. 24). Thus, since the initial stages of industrialization took place earlier in the U.K. than in the U.S.A., the changes in concentration that took place in America between the end of the Civil War and the turn of the century were probably much greater than those occurring in the U.K. over the same period.

In order, therefore, to analyse the relative importance of changes *between* sectors and changes *within* sectors in any shift in the level of overall concentration, data should ideally be available over the relevant time period relating to each sector individually. The importance of this point is well illustrated by referring to American experience over the last eighty years or so. Although far from perfect, the statistical record for the U.S.A. is more detailed than that for the U.K. It is fairly well established, for example, that something approaching a revolution took place in the organization of American manufacturing industry from about 1880 to 1904, when an unsurpassed wave of mergers (reaching its peak during the years 1896 to 1904) largely transformed the sector from one of moderate to low concentration to one dominated by a relatively few giant firms. Broadly speaking, the general pattern of concentration in manufacturing industry in the U.S.A. has remained similar to that created at the turn of the century. The most reliable estimate made at the time (Moody, 1904) suggested that about four-fifths of all existing manufacturing firms were involved in the merger movement which established 318 new organizations controlling about 40 per cent of all the capital in manufacturing industry.

In comparison, concentration in the other sectors (with the possible exception of railways) remained more or less unchanged. Both agriculture, whose relative importance was declining, and distribution remained sectors of low concentration, while public utilities were still relatively unimportant in the economy as well as unconcentrated. Over the period 1905 to about 1935, however, a further substantial increase in concentration in the economy as a whole took place. The largest 200 non-financial firms probably increased their share in the assets of non-financial companies to about one-third compared with something like one-fifth in 1905 (Bain, 1968, p. 108). The important characteristic of this change, however, was that it was mainly due to increases in concentration in the sectors other than manufacturing. The greater part of the change was due to the rapid development of high concentration in the public utility sector whose increase in relative importance in the economy was accompanied by the growth of large firms which were, in the 1920s, caught up in another merger movement.

The position in the manufacturing industry in this period is less clear cut. Some increase in concentration does appear to have taken place but this was fairly slight in comparison with what had occurred at the turn of the century and those changes that did take place were mostly in those parts of manufacturing that were small at the beginning of the period. Thus although overall concentration increased, its significance is only properly understood when the pattern of change in each sector is examined.

Since the mid-1930s, despite some forecasts of concentration increases so large as to lead to serious political and economic consequences if they had occurred, there has been no dramatic change in the level of overall concentration in the U.S.A. Although the share of the largest 150 manufacturing firms in total value added increased from 27 per cent in 1947 to 37 per cent in 1963, this increase appears partly to have made up for ground lost during the war and in the late forties when the share of the largest firms in manufacturing assets actually declined (Bain, 1968, p. 110). In any case the trends in the other sectors have been such as to *reduce* the overall control of assets by the largest companies in the economy, so that whereas in 1933 the largest 200 non-financial enterprises were estimated to control some 55 per cent of all corporate assets, the same proportion were controlled by 300 firms by 1962. Thus overall concentration in the U.S.A. appears to have reached a plateau which has been broadly maintained for about thirty years with little indication of an ever-increasing trend.

Data for the U.K. are, in contrast, relatively sparse for most years before 1935, and the only analyses that have taken place covering an earlier period have concentrated on the whole of the manufacturing, mining and distribution sectors together. A study of particular importance in this connexion is the one by Hart and Prais (1956) covering the period 1885 to 1950. Using for the most part the variance of the logarithms of firm sizes as the measure of concentration (see chapter 3), the study included all public companies with shares quoted on U.K. stock exchanges engaged in mining, manufacturing, and distribution. Thus it excluded the very large numbers of enterprises which were private and unquoted as well as all unincorporated businesses and partnerships. Although it is *now* generally true that public quoted companies include most enterprises which are likely to have any noticeable effect on overall concentration in the manufacturing sector, it was probably far less so in the opening year of the study, 1885. The authors are therefore careful to indicate that the estimates presented for the latter part of the nineteenth century are probably far less reliable guides as to what was happening throughout the sectors studied as a whole than for the later period.

Reference to the size distribution of firms for selected years between 1885 and 1950 showed a distinct rise in overall concentration up to 1939, followed by a fall in 1950 back to a level close to that recorded for 1924. From what has been said in the previous paragraph, one difficulty in interpreting these results is that the actual sectors covered may have varied between the dates studied so that the concentration level towards the end of the period covered a wider sector of the economy than at the beginning. Some check on this possibility is given by further calculations using a constant set of firms throughout the whole period and although the magnitudes of the changes were slightly different the general conclusion of an increase in concentration up to 1939 followed by a subsequent fall, remained unchanged. Some additional confirmation of this general result was given by Hart in a subsequent paper (Hart, 1960, pp. 50–58) which examined the whole corporate sector of manufacturing and distribution (not just the quoted sector) and also the entire private sector (i.e. including partnerships and sole traders). In both cases the data suggested that the share of profits earned by the largest fifty firms increased consistently between 1908 and 1938 but then fell in 1950. Thus although the two studies used different techniques, the first relying on an inequality measure and the second on the more common concentration ratio, both came to the same broad conclusions.

A further interesting result of the first study was the effect that mergers (between quoted companies only) had on the concentration level. The rate of mergers remained stable at around 7 per cent of all companies in each fifteen-year period, and although the concentration level did increase when the effect of mergers was isolated, the change was quite small in comparison with the changes due to the overall growth of firms. In contrast to the highly significant American merger movement at the turn of the century the increased merger activity in parts of the U.K. manufacturing industry at this time was quite insignificant (see Nelson, 1959, Appendix A).

According to Hart and Prais the overall size distribution of firms remained unaffected between 1896 and 1907.

It is possible, however, that mergers have been much more important in the period since 1950 in changing the concentration level in the U.K. Although no systematic study has been made of changes in overall concentration between 1950 and the early 1960s, there are some indications that it has increased, assisted by large-scale mergers. The proportion of assets in the quoted public sector of manufacturing and distribution held by the largest 100 firms appears to have increased from roughly 44 per cent in 1953 to something like 62 per cent by 1963.[1] Over the same period some seventeen of the manufacturing companies ranked in the largest 100 in 1953 were acquired by or merged with other manufacturing companies in the same group. Although it does not necessarily follow, it does seem fairly evident that amongst the largest firms in manufacturing, mergers were a major cause of the increase in concentration. Indeed, concern about the possible harmful effects that unrestricted mergers amongst large firms could have has prompted recent legislation in the U.K., and, incidentally, a tightening also in the policy of the U.S.A.[2]

Despite the noticeable increase in overall concentration in manufacturing industry in the U.S.A. since the Second World War, it seems that for the whole non-financial sector concentration has actually fallen. A comparison with the U.K. over this period is difficult since one of the important sectors which assisted in this decrease in the U.S.A., namely public utilities, was early on brought under public ownership in the U.K. Together with coal mines and the railways, these sectors have thus been much more heavily concentrated in the U.K. since nationalization than in the U.S.A. But in several respects the progress of concentration in the manufacturing sector has been rather similar in both countries. Overall concentration

1. The percentages are estimated from *Company Assets* (1965), National Institute of Economic and Social Research (1955) and National Institute of Economic and Social Research (1956).
2. This legislation is referred to in more detail in chapter 8.

increased in both countries, although at different rates, apparently up until the middle and late 1930s. There then appears to have been some change in the trend during and immediately after the Second World War. In the U.K. smaller companies seem to have grown generally much faster on the average than large companies in this period and the tentative explanation suggested by Hart (1960, p. 55) is that the licensing arrangements in existence during the war guaranteed smaller firms a larger output than they would have obtained in more competitive times. Since 1950 the upward trend has been resumed although apparently at a much faster rate in the U.K. than in the U.S.A. Whether a similar pattern of change has taken place in *market* concentration in the two countries is discussed in the following section.

The Trend in Market Concentration

Most studies which have attempted to measure changes in market concentration have relied upon the concentration ratio calculated from Census data. Thus the shortcomings described in chapter 3 still apply, but in addition the measurement of changes over time involves some additional problems. The first of these difficulties really stems from the limitations of the concentration ratio itself. It was suggested above in chapter 5 that without knowledge of the related size distribution of firms in an industry the concentration ratio told us relatively little about the structure of the industry and its possible behaviour and performance. In the present context, an unchanged 70 per cent share in the industry output held by the three largest firms, although suggesting a stable situation, with the possibility of collusion, may in fact hide considerable dynamism in the industry if the identity of the three largest firms changes continually. In year one, for example, firms A, B and C may hold respectively 30, 20 and 20 per cent of the market. Ten years later the concentration ratio may still show 70 per cent of the market controlled by three firms but if the composition of that aggregate share is now firm B 25 per cent, firm D 25 per cent and firm A 20 per cent, there has evidently been considerable competition for market shares between the largest firms shown not only by the change in rank of the previous leaders but by the emergence of firm D amongst the top three firms.

Usually the identity of the top three firms is unknown. The Census authorities cannot give individual identities because of their disclosure rules. Consequently, little is known for certain of the extent to which unchanged concentration ratios for individual markets do in fact obscure a dynamic situation. It has been established, for the U.K. however, that over a number of years considerable changes both in identity and ranking have taken place amongst the largest manufacturing companies. From an examination of the fifty largest companies ranked according to profits at ten yearly intervals, Hart (1960, p. 56) concluded that before 1924 about one-fifth of the firms fell out of the list for one reason or another, but by 1950 the rate per decade had increased to two-fifths. A comparison of the lists[1] of the largest manufacturing companies ranked by net assets made for the years 1953 and 1963 shows that this level of turnover has been maintained. The evidence for the U.S.A., on the other hand, points to exactly the opposite conclusion. A study of the change in identities and ranking amongst the 100 largest American manufacturing companies for a similar period indicated that the rate of 'entry and exit' to the list had slowed down appreciably since the Second World War (Collins and Preston, 1961).

A difficulty of another kind concerns the changes in definition and scope of industries defined by the Census authorities. Several factors may play a part in the decision to redefine industry boundaries between one Census and the next. The rise of an almost completely new technology may, for example, indicate the need for an entirely new industry classification. Less dramatic may be a change in demand which makes one or two principal products of an industry sufficiently important to merit a separate category. Relatively isolated instances of this kind would probably not affect the Census data sufficiently

1. National Institute of Economic and Social Research (1955) and *Company Assets* (1965).

to impair the study of the change in concentration over time. It is when a fundamental revision is thought necessary which involves the basic definition of a large number of industries that the difficulty becomes formidable. The adoption of the new Standard Industrial Classification in the U.K. for presenting the data of the 1958 Census of Production meant, for example, that only sixty-three out of the total of 120 manufacturing industries were comparable between the years 1951 and 1958. Also those industries that *were* comparable were not amongst the largest, accounting in all for only 39 per cent of total employment in manufacturing industry in 1958 (see Armstrong and Silberston, 1965, p. 403).

It is also possible that substantial changes in the degrees of specialization and exclusiveness for the same industry between two dates can give misleading results as to the actual change in concentration of output of the principal products of the industry that has taken place. This point is best illustrated by referring to the actual example given by Evely and Little (1960, p. 147). A simple comparison of the concentration ratios for the car and taxi industry between 1935 and 1951 suggested a substantial increase in concentration over the period: the three-firm net output concentration ratio increased from 47 per cent to 82 per cent and the employment concentration ratio from 48 per cent to 69 per cent. However, on the basis of certain assumptions it was possible to estimate a *principal product concentration ratio* (i.e. the proportion of output of the principal products of the industry accounted for by the three largest firms) which lay between 30 and 64 per cent in 1935 and between 47 and 55 per cent in 1951. Thus on the basis of these estimates it was impossible to say whether the concentration of output had increased, decreased or remained constant. The reason for the apparent discrepancy between the two results given by the net output or employment ratio and the principal product ratio lay in the reduced degrees of specialization and exclusiveness of the output of the principal products. The degree of specialization fell from 77 per cent in 1935 to 69 per cent in 1951 and the degree of exclusiveness from almost 100 per cent to 69 per cent. These changes meant that the gross output concentration ratio referred only to a relatively small part of the total output of cars and taxis produced in 1951. In fact on the basis of a more detailed examination of additional data of the industry, Evely and Little concluded that the proportion of output of cars and taxis produced by the three largest firms actually fell over the period studied. Ideally, therefore, changes in market concentration over time are best measured by a principal product concentration ratio, but adequate information is rarely available.

As far as the U.K. is concerned little systematic data on market concentration of any kind are available before the year 1935. It is true that Evely and Little (1960, chapter 8) give interesting case studies of the early growth in high concentration in some industries due usually to the development of one or two firms, such as in wallpaper, salt, cement, tobacco products and cotton thread, but this covers only a small fraction of manufacturing industry. For the U.S.A. there are more comprehensive estimates relating to the beginning of the century. One study suggests, for example, that between about 1901 and 1947 the proportion of net output in manufacturing produced by industries with a four-firm concentration ratio of 50 per cent or more fell from just on one-third to just under one-quarter. The accuracy of the data for the earlier year was too doubtful to conclude simply that concentration had decreased over the period. The author was only prepared to suggest that the 'odds are better than even that there has actually been *some* decline in concentration. It is a good bet that there has been no actual increase; and the odds do seem high against any substantial increase' (Adelman, 1958, p. 40).

There has been, furthermore, no strong evidence of any general upward trend in market concentration since 1947. A comparison of manufacturing industries' four-firm concentration ratios between 1947 and 1958 indicated a slight increase in the importance of industries with concentrations of 60 per cent or more and a corresponding decrease in importance for those industries with concentration ratios between 40 and 60 per cent. But the change seems too small to be statistically significant. Although there continue to be important increases in concentration in individual industries in the U.S.A., there is no general indication of a persistent upward trend.

A summary comparison of concentration in the private sector of industry in the U.K. between 1935 and 1951 was made by Evely and Little (1960, p. 64–5). By grouping the percentage of total employment and output in the 220 industry groups according to their employment concentration ratios they were able to show graphically that little change overall had taken place. If anything a slight increase in the sixteen-year period might have occurred, but this could only have been marginal. For example, roughly 10 per cent of total employment was in industries with a concentration ratio of 60 per cent or more in 1935 compared with 12 per cent in 1951. Although a general comparison of this kind avoids the worst of the difficulties when comparisons over time are to be made, a full analysis of change requires a detailed industry-by-industry comparison.

It was possible to estimate principal product concentration ratios for 185 industries for 1935 and 1951. In only one-third of them was any discernible change in the concentration ratio apparent. Out of this total thirty-nine showed an increase and twenty-two a decrease in concentration. For the purposes of their subsequent statistical analysis Evely and Little concentrated on only forty-one of these industries which showed a distinct concentration change since the other twenty did not meet the strict tests of comparability that were laid down. Within the surviving group some twenty-seven industries showed an increase in concentration and fourteen a decrease. There was little difference between the magnitude of the upward changes compared with those in a downward direction and so any general conclusion that market concentration increased over this period has to rest mainly on the *number* of industries showing an increase (almost twice as many as showed a decrease).

It is interesting that in two-thirds of the 185 industries no change in concentration was observed. This bears out the conclusion of the previous section that the war period of government regulation and control helped preserve the market shares of smaller firms against inroads by larger competitors.

The only year after 1951 for which data is available for a large section of the private sector is 1958. Out of the sixty-three industries that could be made comparable between the two years, thirty-six showed some increase in concentration and sixteen a definite decrease. Of the remainder, two industries showed no change and in nine cases it was impossible to determine the direction of change. The industrial sectors particularly affected by increases in concentration appeared to be textiles and food. Compared with 1935 it was found that fewer and larger plants were operating in most industries and in particular that the average size of plant in the largest size group was increasing. It was also apparent that plants were generally operated by fewer firms. Taken together the data on plant sizes and concentration changes indicated that 'the extent to which many industries are dominated by a few "giant" enterprises seems to be increasing' (Armstrong and Silberston, 1965, p. 405).

There is some indication that concentration may well have increased further in many industries since 1958. First, the volume of merger activity since 1961 has generally been much higher than it was in the years before 1958 and although this does not necessarily mean an automatic increase in concentration, where some of the largest firms in an industry are involved, as in the case, for example, of the British Motor Corporation and Leyland, and the General Electric Company and Associated Electrical Industries, the immediate effect is to increase concentration. A second indirect indicator of the continued increase is given by the initial results of the 1963 Census of Production. Amongst the first thirty-nine industries for which data have been published the number of enterprises fell on average by 15 per cent between 1958 and 1963. At the same time the number of enterprises increased in only seven industries (Pratten, 1968, p. 41).

Conclusion

Up to 1950 the trend in overall concentration in manufacturing industry in the U.K. and U.S.A. seems to have been roughly similar. In both countries the upward trend seems to have been reversed somewhat during and immediately after the Second World War. Since then although the overall concentration level has again been increasing in both countries the *rate* of increase appears to have been considerably faster in the U.K. than in the U.S.A. Similarly, since about 1951, there is some indication that market concentration has been increasing noticeably in numerous U.K. manufacturing industries while remaining fairly stable in the U.S.A. Furthermore, the contrasting attitudes of the Governments of the two countries to industrial concentration as reflected in their anti-trust policies seem likely to maintain rather than reduce these differences in the future. This point is taken up again in detail in the concluding chapter.

7 Industrial Concentration and Market Behaviour and Performance

Introduction

It has already been emphasized that the study of industrial concentration, particularly in individual markets, is only a means to an end and not an end in itself. A measure of the level of market concentration is useful only to the extent that it gives a first indication of the kinds of behaviour and performance that can be expected from industry. Ideally, a full specification of *all* relevant structural characteristics of the industry (especially the height of barriers to new entry and the degree of product differentiation, as well as the level of concentration) should be studied before making any predictions as to market behaviour and performance. But except in a few instances data of this kind are unavailable. Even when such details are available, however, it is not an easy matter to determine *a priori* how, for example, prices will be determined or how high the level of profits will be for firms in the industry. For only in the two extreme cases of monopoly and perfect competition does theory give precise indications of the method of price determination and the level of profits to be expected in equilibrium.

It is true that in some practical instances the behaviour of firms has come close to that predicted by theory, and a recent example in the U.K. was given by the Monopolies Commission in their report on the supply of man-made cellulosic fibres. Courtaulds were responsible for about 98 per cent of U.K. production in 1966 and also had the protection of a relatively high tariff. Although cellulosic fibre is subject to competition from other fibres, Courtaulds' position in several respects resembled a textbook monopoly. The Commission were satisfied that 'the production policy pursued by Courtaulds exemplifies one of the classic disadvantages of monopoly, the limitation of supply to the level most advantageous for the producer, which is below the level which would be met in a competitive situation' (Monopolies Commission, 1968). Generally, however, the structure of the industry will not lie particularly close to either extreme. The classification of markets presented in Table 7 (chapter 5) suggests that a large proportion of manufacturing industries contain strong elements of oligopoly where a large variety of methods of price determination are possible.

The purpose of the present chapter, therefore, is briefly to indicate, first, some of the patterns of price behaviour that have been found recently in some of these U.K. industries of medium and high concentration, and second, to illustrate the extent to which measures of concentration are associated with various aspects of market performance, in particular, profitability.

Market Concentration and Market Behaviour

In the discussion that follows two forms of price determination in concentrated industries are mentioned, complete collusion and price leadership. It is essential, however, to bear in mind first that these terms are generic and encompass a wide variety of methods for establishing prices, and second, that although price formation is an important aspect of market behaviour, other aspects, such as the determination of selling costs and the rate of product change, are also important but are not dealt with here.

Once we move away from industries having low concentration and other structural characteristics that bring them close to the perfectly competitive model, prices cease to be determined 'externally' to the individual firms in the industry and are generally either set jointly by the firms following consultation (usually termed 'collusion' in this context), or individually by firms who have tried to take account of the reaction of rivals to their decision. In both cases the central feature of the process is the interdependence of firms in the industry.

Most forms of collusive arrangements have been illegal in the U.S.A. since the passage of the first anti-trust laws around the turn of the century, but it has only been in the last twenty years or so that investigation and control of such agreements has brought to light details of their extent and variety in the U.K. Most of the cases heard by the Restrictive Practices Court[1] have involved highly developed agreements between manufacturers and can be termed 'completely collusive'. Three conditions have to be fulfilled for collusion to be complete: all producers in the industry have to be members; the terms of the agreement are strictly adhered to by all members; and the terms of agreement (which may cover both prices and output quotas) are free from ambiguity (Bain, 1968, p. 307). An interesting example of a very effective agreement of this kind where all of these conditions were present, was that adopted by the Cement Manufacturers Federation for fixing the price of cement in the U.K. When the agreement was examined by the Restrictive Practices Court in 1961 the nine members of the Federation produced virtually all of the country's cement and the four largest firms were responsible for 85 per cent of the total output. The largest firm dominated the industry with a market share of 65 per cent. The Federation had determined prices in the industry since 1934 and this involved dividing the country into eleven regions within each of which delivered prices were laid down in a separate price schedule. Associated with the price fixing arrangements were schemes for determining margins for merchants and aggregated rebates to be allowed to different kinds of customers. Any members desiring an upward or downward adjustment of prices had to put their proposal before a meeting of the Federation. Although there were many other interesting features of this agreement, in the present context it is mentioned mainly as an important illustration of how detailed and rigorous price fixing can be in a highly concentrated industry. There

1. The role of the Court is discussed in more detail in chapter 8.

was no evidence of any significant sales made on terms other than those laid down in the agreement and no examples of recalcitrant firms breaking away from the Federation in an attempt to improve their market share. Undoubtedly the strength of the leading producer had played a great part in the continuous stability of the scheme. In fact the existing size distribution of firms in the industry influenced the Court to some extent in giving judgement in favour of the price agreement. It concluded that if the agreement were made void the natural result would not be price competition but price leadership under the auspices of the dominant producer. In other words the smaller firms in the industry would simply follow the pattern of prices and price changes established by the price leader without regard to their own cost levels. This possibility seemed all the more likely in the cement industry where consultation, long required by the formal price agreement, was almost bound to continue on only a slightly less formal basis if the agreement were to be abandoned.

It is interesting to note that this tacit form of collusion (i.e. price leadership) did follow close on the heels of the abandonment of a formal price agreement in the cables industry in the U.K. At the time of these developments (1959–60) there were more than thirty cable producers, the largest two of which controlled about 70 per cent of the total output. Following adverse comments on its price and output quota agreements by the Monopolies Commission (1952), the industry at first modified and then voluntarily terminated the majority of its price fixing arrangements. This was followed by a short period of intense price competition when rivalry between the leading firms resulted in a 20 per cent reduction in prices.[1] Within a few months of the ending of the agreements, however, two strategically timed price *increases* by one of the leading producers, British Insulated Callender's Cables, were followed by rival firms and the period of price instability brought to an end, although at a considerably lower level of prices than had existed before.

1. For a detailed account of the results of ending this and other restrictive agreements see Heath (1961).

Although tacit collusion in the form of price leadership appears to suffer from many of the disadvantages of a more formal, documented agreement (individual firms' prices may not reflect their costs, for example), it is difficult to see what other system of price determination in highly concentrated industries could bring about better economic results. In the U.S.A. where formal agreements have not been legally possible for many years, price leadership is a very common practice (Bain, 1968, p. 312). On balance this is probably to be preferred in many instances since it is likely to provide more opportunities for 'hidden' price competition in the form, for example, of special terms to individual customers below the leader's declared price levels. This, of course, is even more likely to occur where the recognized price leader is not the most efficient producer, as was true in the British rubber footwear industry where Dunlop owed its leadership position apparently to its overall size and financial strength rather than to its comparative efficiency in production (Monopolies Commission, 1956a). Price leadership is also unlikely to be accompanied by arrangements covering such things as exclusive dealing and aggregated rebates which can play an important part in impeding entry to an industry and thus neutralize one of the most powerful constraints on the behaviour of existing firms.

An interesting feature of some of the cases heard before the Restrictive Practices Court has been the considerable variation in the *number* of firms that could successfully be included in formal price fixing arrangements. It was suggested in chapter 5 above that oligopoly theory gave little assistance in determining the level of concentration and number of firms necessary to produce a given pattern of price behaviour. Furthermore, it is usually suggested that complete collusion is only practical where the number of firms is relatively small. Yet effective price agreements had been maintained in manufacturing industries like carpet production with as many as fifty-eight members and in the production of nuts and bolts with forty-four members. The defence of an agreement in the Court is not taken up lightly by a trade association because of the expense and time involved and therefore those heard are likely to be considered beneficial by the firms concerned. It is thus evident that detailed collusion can work where the number of firms is large. To the extent, therefore, that such formal collusion is allowed to continue concentration measures alone will give a poor indication of the likely conduct of the industry. On the other hand, judging from U.S.A. experience, the abandonment of many price agreements that has taken place in the U.K. over the last few years may well lead to the spread of price leadership among the affected industries.

Market Concentration and Market Performance

Amongst the more important aspects of industrial performance are: 'technical' performance, relating to the extent that products are manufactured in plants and firms of an efficient size; 'allocative' performance, relating to the long-run association between prices and marginal costs, as reflected in profit margins; 'innovation' performance, which includes the relative success with which industries seek out and adopt new processes and products; and 'promotional' performance, which will be reflected in the ratio of selling costs to costs of production.

Price theory gives its clearest predictions about one aspect of market performance in particular, i.e. 'allocative' performance. One of its central conclusions is that the allocation of resources, when monopoly is present in some industries, is distorted since in such industries price will be above marginal cost, output will be restricted and long-run excess profits will be earned. This implies that too few resources are devoted to the production of the monopolized goods and too many resources are employed elsewhere. To the extent, therefore, that industries of high market concentration approach the behaviour of monopolists a similar performance may be expected. In practical terms this suggests that the higher the level of market concentration, the greater the likely divergence in the long run between prices and marginal costs or (on the assumption that generally firms are able to operate on a horizontally shaped average cost curve, in which case marginal and average costs coincide) between prices and average costs. This divergence will be reflected in a long-run profit rate in excess of the 'normal' return on capital and will imply some degree of output restriction. If high levels of market concentration are also associated with high barriers to entry these tendencies are likely to be reinforced. On the other hand if the entry barriers are lower for industries of high concentration than for industries of moderate concentration, it is possible that the entry conditions in the former industries will keep prices (and hence profits) as low as in the latter, despite the level of concentration.

Testing the hypothesis of the direct relationship between profit rates and concentration level, however, is difficult, even assuming that adequate data are available from firms relating to their operations in individual industries, rather than to several different industries. Excess profits may derive from several different sources and only one of these may strictly speaking be associated with the concentration level. In the short run, for example, unexpected changes in demand or cost conditions may result in firms in some industries earning higher than the long-run normal rate. At the same time and for the same reasons other firms in different industries may be earning less than normal profits. But these results are to be expected as part of the market adjustment process under uncertainty whatever the level of concentration.

Some excess profit is justifiable on the grounds that the firms concerned have undertaken exceptional risks by developing and introducing new products or processes. Since the promotion of the 'new' generally carries with it far more uncertainty about the ultimate return (as indicated in chapter 2 above) than simply the continued production of a well-tried product, it is often suggested that the prospect of an above-normal profit is required to provide the stimulus to such innovation. Here again, though, this may give an explanation for *periodic* excess profits by some firms (as well as losses by firms whose innovations are unsuccessful), but it cannot account for uninterrupted long-term excess profits. The latter can only be fully explained by the existence of monopolistic market power which allows the restriction of output, and to the extent that high concentration reflects such power then persistent excess profits are to be expected.

The Monopolies Commission has frequently commented on the profit record of firms holding a dominant position in their industry, although by the end of 1968 in only eight cases out of a total of twenty-three dominant firms investigated was the rate of return considered high enough to be against the public interest. In two of its earlier reports (on the supply of matches and the supply of industrial and medical gases) the Commission took particular exception to persistently high rates of return earned by near monopolies both of whom had taken active steps to eliminate competition and who appeared to operate under conditions of low risk. In another case, while it accepted that the dominant firm, The Champion Sparking Plug Company (in the report on Electrical Equipment for Motor Vehicles) was efficient, the Commission was nevertheless dissatisfied with the company's exceptionally high rate of return because its market power gave it considerable discretion over its own price and profit levels so that 'to retain over a long period so large a measure of the rewards of efficiency has been objectionable'. Where, however, high profits were consistently earned in the face of considerable competition and largely as a result of the company's skill in developing and applying new techniques, the Commission saw no danger to the public interest. The company in question was the Molins Machine Company Ltd, a manufacturer of cigarette and tobacco processing machinery, which at the time of the investigation in 1961 supplied about 55 per cent of the market. On the other hand, in a more recent case high profits earned despite fierce competition were condemned by the Commission as excessive. The competition, it is true, was of a different kind to that encountered by Molins for it took the form of product differentiation and heavy sales promotion. In fact, in this report on the supply of detergents the Commission concluded that it was largely as a result of this competition that profits could remain so high. They argued that the heavy volume of sales expenditure sustained over a long period acted as an effective barrier to new entry to the industry and therefore shielded the high profits earned even by the less efficient of the two duopolists.

Dominant firms in some other industries earned more modest rewards and although the Commission sometimes viewed this as a result of the restraint of firms with considerable market power it was fully aware that it could equally signify lethargy and lack of enterprise. As we would expect, therefore, the reports of the Commission have shown not only a considerable range of profits earned by dominant firms but also that high profits can derive from a number of sources.

A detailed study of a cross section of industries may, on the other hand, be expected to provide a more satisfactory test of the relationship between the concentration level and profitability. Unfortunately, although several extensive studies of this hypothesis have been made for the U.S.A., there has so far been only one published concerned with U.K. manufacturing industry. In this study Hart found no support for the hypothesis that rates of return vary directly with the level of concentration (Hart, 1968, pp. 258–64). Neither in a sample of thirty-seven industries nor for forty-six leading firms was there any significant difference between average profitability in industries of high concentration compared with those of medium or low concentration. Similar results were found by Stigler in an extensive analysis involving a wide cross-section of U.S. manufacturing industries covering the periods 1938–41 and 1951–7 (Stigler, 1963, p. 67).

On the other hand, there is some positive evidence to show that although there may not be a *continuous* relationship between profitability and concentration level, there may be a critical level above which average profitability is higher than in industries of moderate or low concentration. Bain, for example, established such a relationship in a carefully selected sample of forty-two U.S. manufacturing industries. He found that average profitability over the period 1936–40 was significantly higher in industries where the eight-firm concentration ratio was over 70 per cent, compared with those where the ratio was less than 70 per cent (Bain, 1951). Yet within each group of industries there was no consistent relationship between profit rates and concentration level.[1] This result is consistent with the suggestion that there are two broad categories of oligopoly (see chapter 5, above): one consisting of a relatively few important firms who are able to maintain a consistent and collusive policy of joint profit maximization which results in long-run profits above normal, and the other, including those industries of moderate or low concentration, in which one or two fairly large firms exist side by side with a number of smaller firms where collusive behaviour (in the face of a strong anti-trust policy) is less stable and as a consequence long-run profits are closer to the competitive level. There is as yet certainly insufficient evidence to conclude that this relationship between concentration and profitability is established for a wide range of industries, but one result that has found general agreement among most studies is that industries of high concentration are less likely to earn very low rates of return and also suffer less fluctuations over time in their profit rate.

It was mentioned in chapter 2 that considerable attention has been focused recently on what may be called the 'innovation' performance of industries, or their record in discovering and applying new production methods which lead to a saving in real resources. The issues of firm size and market structure in relation to innovation performance have received special notice despite the fact that the measurement of this dimension of performance poses rather special problems for the investigator. Lacking systematic data on the 'output' of inventions and innovations, most studies have instead considered information on the input side such as the amounts spent on research and development (R and D), and the number of patents filed, although there need not be any strict relationship between the two. In other words, there is no *a priori* reason to expect that the firms which spend the highest proportion of their sales revenue on R and D or take out the greatest number of patents will

1. Similar results for the post-war period have also been found by Bain (1956, chapter 7), and Mann (1966).

achieve the most 'progressive' performance. On the other hand, there is now available sufficient data, particularly on recent R and D expenditures, to give at least a preliminary answer to some of the more interesting questions.

Firstly, a recent comparison between the U.S.A. and the U.K. concluded that R and D expenditures in the whole private industrial sector were equally concentrated amongst a relatively small group of large firms: roughly 350 firms accounted for about 85 per cent of the total in both countries. Despite the smaller absolute size on average of the U.K. firms it seemed unlikely that they suffered any handicap from diseconomies of small scale as a result (Freeman, 1962).

The second point is more strictly related to market concentration and is particularly interesting since it involves a comparison of the R and D efforts of similar industries in the two different countries rather than the relative records of different industries in the same country which may be at quite different phases in their development and have varying degrees of technological complexity and thus be faced with different opportunities for innovation. A comparison of the ratio of R and D expenditures to sales for seventeen manufacturing industries in the U.K. and the U.S.A. found generally little difference between the two countries. The industries were grouped into three classes ranked according to their degree of research intensity and in the first two groups little or no difference in comparative performance was observed while in the third, more technologically stagnant group, the U.K. seemed to concentrate more research effort than the U.S.A. However, as the author of the study concluded, since seller concentration in both Britain and America is on the average lower in the third group than in the other two 'these data offer no broad-gauged support for the view that Britain needs more mergers or more monopoly in order to promote R and D expenditure' (Caves (ed.), 1968, p. 299). In contrast, a recent policy document in the U.K. took almost the directly opposite view (White Paper, 1966), and the present government has initiated various policies which are likely to have an important effect on concentration levels.

Yet, as we have tried to indicate in the present chapter, the systematic evidence available on certain aspects of market behaviour and performance in relation to industrial concentration is far from giving clear-cut guides to the policy-maker.

8 Policy Approaches to Industrial Concentration

Introduction

It has only been in the last twenty years that the U.K. has had any permanent machinery for the investigation and control of industrial concentration. In contrast, anti-trust policy in the U.S.A. dates from the passage of the Sherman Act in 1890. The reasons for this comparatively late development of British policy are not difficult to find. Around the turn of the century when the emergence of 'trusts' and their dubious competitive methods in the U.S.A. had aroused sufficient public concern for the foundations of a strong anti-trust policy to be laid, British industry, although by no means as free from pricing agreements as is sometimes claimed, was still highly competitive. On the one hand, a large proportion of the output of the staple industries was sold in foreign markets where it was difficult to restrain competition, and on the other hand the continuance of the traditional policy of free trade severely constrained the price-fixing arrangements of domestic producers, subject to competition from imports. At the same time, although dominant firms were already emerging in some industries (e.g. cement, tobacco and soap) especially by merging with other enterprises, the merger movement in the U.K. probably had a much slighter impact than similar developments in the U.S.A. (see chapter 6).

In the inter-war period, stagnation in the traditional staple industries with the emergence of widespread excess capacity made price fixing arrangements impossible to maintain. This imbalance in industrial structure at a time of world depression was hardly the time to develop a policy aimed at maintaining competition and preventing the emergence of monopoly power. Indeed the Government saw its role as one of encouraging the 'rationalization' of industry which involved the mutual co-operation of all firms in eliminating excess capacity. In some industries arrangements were introduced for stabilizing prices and allocating output quotas, so that 'by the outbreak of the Second World War it is probable that the majority of the leading British industries were familiar with devices for restricting competition' (Allen, 1968, p. 55). It was also true, of course, that in the face of severe depression similar developments took place in the U.S.A., particularly under the provisions of the National Industrial Recovery Act which formulated codes of 'fair competition' to be administered by industrial trade associations.

During the Second World War the close controls required over prices, production and imports all helped to lessen the pressures of competition while the close co-operation of the Government with dominant firms and trade associations helped further to entrench their positions. It was thus by no means a foregone conclusion that after the war policy should be directed at investigating positions of market dominance or dismantling agreements between firms which by then had been actively encouraged by the Government for more than a decade. Only the continued high level of employment bringing problems of a different kind and the revelations about the effects of certain restrictive practices in some of the earlier reports of the Monopolies Commission persuaded the Government in the U.K. that a positive anti-trust policy had an important part to play in improving the performance of British industry.

In the present context it is convenient to discuss various phases of this policy under three separate headings: the investigation and control of high levels of concentration, the attempt to forestall undesirable increases in concentration that could occur through mergers, and the control of the various devices used by groups of firms on occasion to preserve existing levels of concentration for their own advantage.

High Levels of Concentration

The Monopolies and Restrictive Practices (Inquiry and Control) Act, 1948, was the first statute of modern times in the U.K. to provide permanent machinery for the investigation of moderate and high levels of industrial concentration. The body established for this purpose, the Monopolies Commission, was an independent tribunal which, on reference by the Board of Trade, investigated the supply or processing of goods for the domestic or export markets where at least one-third of the goods was supplied by a single firm or by two or more firms through an arrangement for restricting competition. In the present section we are only concerned with the 'single firm' case (and in any event since 1956 restrictive agreements have been investigated by a different body, the Restrictive Practices Court). Specifically excluded from the original Act were the nationalized industries and trade unions as well as services (although a revision to the law in 1965 makes it possible for the latter to be investigated by the Commission).

It is evident that the criterion of *one-third* of the total supply is a fairly arbitrary quantity settled on rather out of statutory convenience than strict economic reasoning. As has been suggested in previous chapters, there is little ground given by economic theory for expecting different market behaviour and performance to follow from an industry where one firm controls 33 per cent of the output as against one where it controls 40 or 50 per cent. However, there is no presumption in the Act *against* any firm controlling one-third or more of the market and the criterion does give broad scope for inquiries into a wide range of industries where monopolistic or oligopolistic behaviour is most likely to be found. The investigations of the Commission fall generally into three phases: first, it determines whether one-third or more of the total supply is in fact in the hands of a single producer; second, it examines the practices of the industry and reports on the extent to which 'things done' by the firms were a natural result of the 'monopolistic' structure of the industry and the extent to which they have been used for the purpose of preserving the monopoly; and third, it decides whether the 'things done' have operated or may operate against the public interest and makes recommendations, if necessary, as to how the situation could be improved. Any action taken as a result of a report of the Commission lies in the hands of the Board of Trade which frequently has obtained an undertaking from the firms concerned in line with the Commission's proposals.

Although the Commission is expected to make judgements as to whether certain policies by dominant firms are in the public interest, the 1948 Act gave very little guidance on how such assessments were to be made. Indeed, a past member of the Commission has recently commented that 'the guidance given by the Act consisted of a string of platitudes which the Commission found valueless' (Allen, 1968, p. 66). There is nothing in the Act to suggest that competition is more desirable than monopoly or that some specific practices or 'things done' are more harmful than others.

It is interesting to note here that the fundamental pillar of American anti-trust policy, the Sherman Act, despite its far greater influence on the structure of American industry than the Monopolies Commission on British industry, also says nothing about desirable forms of market structure or behaviour. It created two types of offence: restraint of trade and monopolizing or attempts to monopolize, and thus appears (like the Monopolies Commission) to be concerned with behaviour rather than monopoly or size as such.

In both countries one aspect of policy in relation to highly concentrated industries has caused particular difficulty. This concerns the feasible remedies that can be applied to an industry where the market dominance of one or two firms with demonstrable economies of scale has been accompanied by practices which in the U.K. are found to be against the public interest and in the U.S.A. have amounted to monopolization or a restriction of competition. One possibility is the break up of the dominant enterprises into two or more units which then act independently.[1] Even in the context of the very large American market, however, where such a measure may seem viable without loss of scale economies, there has been considerable reluctance to employ it since the famous dissolution of the Standard Oil and American Tobacco trusts following the decisions of the Supreme Court in 1911. In two more recent cases, for example, where monopolistic firms were found to have violated the Sherman Act less drastic remedies were adopted. The Aluminium Company of America (Alcoa) avoided dissolution in 1945 because the Government disposed of its aluminium producing capacity built up during the war to two new producers which the Court were satisfied would provide effective competition. Similarly, although the United Shoe Machinery Co. was found to have used its market dominance to limit actual and exclude potential competition, the remedy adopted was to ensure that the offending company used more liberal policies in relation to its customers than hitherto (e.g. the company had to undertake amongst other things to sell its machines when customers wished to buy rather than lease).

A clear example of this dilemma was given by the Monopolies Commission report on the supply of industrial and medical gases where the dominant firm, British Oxygen, came very close to the textbook case of pure monopoly. Despite its scale advantages British Oxygen had engaged in a series of measures deliberately designed to exclude competition, such as taking over rival companies, controlling the supply of equipment, and using fighting companies to undermine other producers. In addition it was found that the company had charged excessively high prices (Rowley, 1966, pp. 337–9). Of the dominant firm investigations made so far, the case for a radical remedy was probably strongest in this industry and in fact a minority of the Commission suggested that the company should be nationalized. But the majority recom-

1. Before the change in the law in 1965 this remedy would have required a special Act of Parliament and thus probably played some part in the Monopolies Commission's attitude to this possibility.

mendation was neither for nationalization nor dissolution but proposed a biennial review of prices, profits and costs. This view, however, was not shared by the Board of Trade which was satisfied that a number of undertakings given by British Oxygen would ensure that no further abuse of its monopoly position would take place in the future. Furthermore, on the only occasion when the Monopolies Commission has recommended a divestiture of shares in order to safeguard future competition in an oligopolistic industry (Monopolies Commission, 1961), the Board of Trade also refused to take up the suggestion but was again content with an assurance from the dominant firm that it would not interfere with the policy of its major domestic rival in which it had a hitherto undisclosed and substantial shareholding. Thus the Commission has been loath to recommend dissolution or even divestiture and in any case the Board of Trade has seemed very unreceptive to any very radical suggestions.

The examples quoted are, of course, extreme in the sense that the structure of the industry and the accompanying actual or potential restraints on competition were seen as especially harmful. In other cases, where firms have been equally dominant in their respective markets, the Commission has been satisfied with recommendations of a less revolutionary kind such as the abolition of resale price maintenance (in the reports on the supply of equipment for motor vehicles, of pneumatic tyres and of wallpaper), and in the case of two dominant firms, Imperial Chemical Industries (in the supply of chemical fertilizers) and Pilkington Brothers (in the supply of flat glass) none of the policies were found to operate or be likely to operate against the public interest.

It is important, nevertheless, that positive measures should be available for ensuring a degree of competition in those industries where market dominance has been or is likely to be accompanied by monopolistic practices. This is particularly pressing for the U.K. where balance-of-payments problems are likely to place an effective bar on selective tariff cuts as a remedy. In two cases the Commission has made such a recommendation: in the reports on the supply of colour film and cellulosic fibre, but there is little chance of this being accepted by the Board of Trade.[1] For this reason measures designed to prevent undesirable increases in concentration by merger seem to deserve special emphasis.

Merger Policy and Industrial Concentration

We have already seen that the latter part of the 1950s and early 1960s displayed a substantial rise in the number and importance of mergers between firms in U.K. manufacturing industry (see chapter 6). In addition, although the Monopolies Commission had only recommended that a dominant firm should actually cease merger activity in one case, that of the Wallpaper Manufacturers Company, it had made it fairly clear that it disliked the past merger record of other large firms such as the British Oxygen Company, Imperial Tobacco, British Match Corporation and Chloride Electrical Storage Company. The time was evidently ripe for an extension of policy into the field of merger investigation and control. This was provided by the Monopolies and Mergers Act passed in 1965, although it had been foreshadowed to a large extent by a White Paper (1964) on monopoly policy published by the previous government, so there was a large measure of agreement between the two main political parties on the central issues.

According to the Act the powers of the Board of Trade and the scope of inquiry by the Monopolies Commission were both considerably increased. The Board can refer mergers to the Commission where the assets to be acquired are valued at over £5 million or where an existing monopoly (as defined in the earlier Act of 1948) would be increased. Moreover, it was given power to delay any merger which it has asked the Commission to investigate and following a recommendation from the Commission can prohibit a merger or even break up an existing monopoly.[2]

1. In the case of colour film the Board has already rejected the suggestion and it has also intimated that the same holds for cellulosic fibre.
2. These are the main features which are relevant to the present

The pragmatic approach used by the Monopolies Commission before the 1965 Act is evidently to be continued. In other words, there is no presumption that a proposed merger is against the public interest and there is no implication that certain kinds of mergers are likely to be more harmful than others. Indeed, it was evident at the time of passage of the Act that the Government was fully aware of the advantages that many mergers can bring particularly in the direction of greater economies of scale in the fields of marketing and research and development. The Monopolies Commission itself had commented favourably on the economies of scale achieved through mergers both by Lucas and Smiths in the production of electrical equipment for motor vehicles and by I.C.I. and Fisons in the supply of chemical fertilizers. Nevertheless, it had also been made aware of the harm that could flow from the small residual of mergers that merely increased concentration and the possibility of prolonged monopolistic policies.

It is also interesting that there is special provision in the Act to investigate mergers that do not necessarily increase market concentration but which may increase overall concentration. By allowing the Monopolies Commission to inquire into proposed mergers which simply involve the acquisition of assets of more than £5 million there is specific recognition that an increase in absolute size effected by mergers having vertical or conglomerate aspects may be undesirable. Some of the possible sources of inefficiency or market power that can result from large size (without necessarily involving monopoly in the usual sense) were discussed at the beginning of chapter 6, above, and it is significant that mergers of this kind have increasingly exercised the American anti-trust authorities in recent years. For example, the central provisions of the 1950 Celler Act (which was designed to correct various defects of the Clayton Act passed in 1914)

context, although the Act also contained provisions for the investigation of newspaper mergers, brought services within the province of the Commission and empowered the Board of Trade to control prices and insist on the publication of price lists.

made any merger illegal if its effect was substantially to lessen competition or to tend to create a monopoly. All kinds of mergers were included in the measure, which can be used to stop a single merger or a series of mergers that may have no apparent monopolistic effect in themselves but where there may be an 'incipient tendency' or a 'reasonable probability' that competition may be reduced. Thus if a merger was one of a series of individually unimportant mergers which could have the cumulative effect of substantially lessening competition in the future it would probably be declared illegal. A brief reference to some recent decisions will given an idea of the extent to which any form of concentration increase by merger is circumscribed by a rigorous interpretation of the Clayton Act.

A decision in 1958 on the proposed horizontal merger between the second and fifth largest steel firms made it clear that even where there were demonstrable benefits in the form of enhanced competition in one area of the American market, the merger was illegal since it reduced the number of competitors and the number of independent sources of supply for steel consumers. At present the attitude of the Court to horizontal mergers seems to be that only mergers between small firms which allow them to compete on better terms with existing dominant firms or involving an ailing enterprise on the verge of bankruptcy will not offend the law, consequently there is unlikely to be any substantial increase in market concentration from this source.

The possibility of a reduction in competition is most clearly determined where horizontal mergers are concerned, particularly where they involve some of the largest firms in the industry. But other decisions have made it likely that a large number of vertical and conglomerate mergers will also be found to 'lessen competition'. The acquisition by a shoe manufacturer, for example, of the largest remaining independent shoe retailer was declared illegal even though both sections of the industry had low levels of concentration. In essence the decision rested on the inevitable foreclosure of competition in the retail section of the trade that accompanied the vertical merger, rather than on the size of the market share involved. (For a discussion of this case see Martin, 1963.) Another decision, in 1967, seems likely to forestall mergers between companies which neither have a buyer-seller relationship nor compete in the same market but which see certain scale advantages in marketing related products. The merger between a leading soap producer and the largest producer of domestic bleach was declared illegal since it threatened to reduce competition in the bleach industry. It was argued that the products of the merging bleach firm would be promoted through the enormous advertising budget of the soap firm and this could deter potential entrants to the bleach industry and also put specialist bleach firms at a disadvantage.

Although there are no statistics showing the extent to which decisions such as these have deterred other firms from initiating mergers, there can be little doubt that many which would lead directly to an increase in market or even overall concentration are barely considered. Given the present state of merger policy in the U.S.A., it is also likely that some mergers which would have yielded net benefits do not take place.

From the different anti-trust traditions and in the context of the smaller British market it was not to be expected that a merger policy on American lines would evolve as a result of the new powers of the Monopolies Commission. In the comparatively short time that has elapsed since the passage of the Monopolies and Mergers Act in 1965 ten proposed mergers have been referred to the Commission out of the first 250 or so examined by the Board of Trade (see Rowley, 1968). In three cases the Commission has decided that the proposed merger would be likely to operate against the public interest and on each occasion the Board of Trade has accepted their view and the merger was dropped. Leaving aside the two references involving newspaper mergers which raised rather different, essentially political issues, the predominant characteristic of all but one of the remaining eight mergers was the fairly clear-cut increase in market concentration that would result.[1] This issue was involved in the three cases where the Commission found the merger proposal likely to operate against the public interest and particularly emphasis was put in their judgements on the reduction of competition that was likely to result together with the possibility of increased prices. One of the two investigations so far that has involved vertical integration was of the merger between the largest British motor manufacturer, the British Motor Corporation (B.M.C.) and the largest independent producer of car bodies, Pressed Steel. At the time of the merger Pressed Steel supplied about 40 per cent of B.M.C. car body requirements but almost all of those for Rootes (one of the then 'big five' producers) and two smaller, specialist, manufacturers, Rover and Jaguar. There was on the face of it, therefore, clearly a danger of 'a lessening of competition' (to adopt the American phrase) in the market for car bodies if the merger was allowed. Although fully alive to this danger the Commission was prepared to accept that the merger would be in the public interest subject to an assurance from B.M.C. that it would continue to supply the requirements of Pressed Steel's other customers, its own competitors. In reaching this conclusion the Commission was undoubtedly influenced both by the continued upward trend of concentration in the quest for economies of scale in the motor industry, both in the U.K. and in Europe generally, and by existing levels of integration in this industry in the U.S.A. and the Common Market.

It is generally realized that mergers pose particular difficulties for the policymaker in the field of the regulation of industrial structure. Many mergers can involve both benefits and detriments but their relative importance has to be assessed not on the basis of past experience (as in the case, for example, of an existing dominant firm) but in the light of speculation about such complex issues as the future state of competition, of demand and the rate of technological change. In the U.K.

1. It is interesting that despite the essentially horizontal nature of several of the cases the net assets criterion was used in making the reference to the Commission rather than the 'one-third of the market' criterion.

these problems have if anything been increased by an ambiguity in Government policy. The establishment of the Industrial Reorganization Corporation (I.R.C.) in 1966, shortly after the passage of the Monopolies and Mergers Act, was seen as a means of promoting greater concentration and 'rationalization' in many areas of British industry in order to improve its efficiency and international competitiveness. Probably the most important part of its activities so far has been the initiation of and assistance in mergers involving some of the largest firms in British manufacturing industry, particularly the acquisition by General Electric of Associated Electrical Industries in 1967 and the merger between the Leyland Motor Corporation and British Motor Holdings in 1968. Where the I.R.C. is known to be participating in a merger there is usually an assurance that it will not be referred to the Monopolies Commission. Although there is not necessarily any inconsistency in these two approaches to the merger problem, there does seem to be a need for some means of public scrutiny of mergers amongst very large firms promoted by the I.R.C. so that the possible drawbacks from increased concentration can be aired as well as the widely publicised potential advantages.

Restrictive Practices to Preserve Existing Concentration Levels

Where the law allows firms in an industry to arrange amongst themselves the terms on which they will trade and even the sanctions that will be used collectively against any distributor or customer who does not comply with these conditions, one effect is likely to be the maintenance of the prevailing level of concentration. Where, for example, there is an agreement to share industry output amongst existing firms on a quota basis there may be little scope for an efficient firm to increase its market share (in the calico printing industry, for example, which had been successfully operating such a scheme until a Monopolies Commission investigation in 1954, any member exceeding his quota paid a sum into a central fund). Quota schemes are usually supplemented by additional agreements on prices and the limitation of capacity in the industry, but unless there are barriers to entry the prices fixed are unlikely to be maintained for long above the competitive level (Monopolies Commission, 1954).

It is quite possible, however, that adequate protection from new competition can be preserved by an agreement among existing firms on 'collective discrimination'. This term was the title of a report by the Monopolies Commission which had an important influence on the development of British anti-trust policy. Broadly speaking, the term refers to agreements between firms: to operate a collective boycott against distributors and customers who do not agree to their conditions of sale; to operate exclusive dealing arrangements whereby the associated firms only supply customers who have given an undertaking to purchase solely from members of the agreement; and to give aggregated rebates based on a customer's total purchases from *any* member of the agreement. The possible inefficiencies that can flow from the operation of such arrangements are fully documented in the report (Monopolies Commission, 1955), but in the present context the most important conclusion was that producers independent of the agreement may have great difficulty in entering the industry through the lack of distribution channels, (see also the quotation from the report in chapter 2, above, p. 32) while the collective selection of favoured traders, for exclusive selling or buying or for sales on preferential terms '. . . can easily lead to the creation of a privileged group, subject to relatively little outside competition' (Monopolies Commission, 1955, para. 235). So at both the production and distribution stages of the industry existing concentration levels are likely to be preserved.

A direct outcome of the report on collective discrimination was the Restrictive Trades Practices Act (1956) which provides the machinery of control over a large number of types of restrictive agreements. Firstly, discriminatory practices outlined above employed collectively to enforce resale price maintenance (such as collective boycotts, exclusive dealing and the use of secret trade courts) were made illegal by the 1956 Act.[1] Secondly, a wide range of restrictive agreements (covering, for example, prices, quotas, loyalty rebates and restrictions on capacity) had to be registered in detail with the Registrar of Restrictive Trade Practices who was also responsible for initiating proceedings on individual agreements in the newly established Restrictive Practices Court (see Stevens and Yamey, 1965). The procedure to be followed by the Court as laid down in the Act involved a considerable departure from the legal attitude to restrictive agreements adopted hitherto. The Court proceeds on the assumption that agreements are *against* the public interest and should be prohibited. The onus of showing that the restriction should be maintained lies squarely with the defendants, members of the agreement. They can attempt to do this by convincing the Court that the restriction fulfills one or more of seven conditions[2]. But even if they are successful at this phase of the proceedings the defendants may still fail to win a favourable judgement since the Court then has to balance the advantages flowing from the agreement against any detriment to the public.

By the end of the ten-year period following the passage of the Act more than 2500 agreements had been registered but about 1900 of these had either been abandoned or allowed to expire without reference to the Court. Of the 280 which had been referred some 216 had been settled by mid-1966, although the greater proportion of settlements were made outside the Court (see Rowley, 1968, p. 45). In fact, by November 1966 the Court had heard thirty-three cases and

1. Although resale price maintenance by an individual firm was allowed by the 1956 Act, new legislation in 1964, the Resale Prices Act, has put this practice very much in the same position as restrictive agreements which became registrable under the 1956 Act.
2. It can be argued that an agreement is necessary because (a) the public derives a benefit from it; (b) it protects the public from injury; (c) it offsets the restrictive practices of another trade association; (d) it enables producers to deal with a monopoly buyer; (e) exports or (f) employment would suffer if it were abandoned; (g) it maintains another restriction upheld by the Court.

in only eleven of these had it found in favour of the restrictive agreement.

Taken by themselves these figures might suggest that a dramatic change has taken place in recent years in the competitive conditions under which firms in many industries operate. This would place however too much faith in the power of competition to re-establish itself after a relatively long period of absence. In many industries it is likely that alternative forms of behaviour producing similar results have replaced the restrictive agreements. It was indicated in the previous chapter for example, that price leadership is likely to take the place of a more formal undertaking. Another device which has apparently become widespread has been the 'open price' or 'information' agreement whereby firms undertake to notify each other through their trade association of their prices, discounts, sales and costs. These are circulated throughout the industry in the expectation that all firms will adjust their own policies in the light of the information supplied. Decisions by the Court had left in some doubt the question of whether such agreements were registrable, though their effect may be to eliminate competition. Further legislation, however, which would bring information agreements within the authority of the Restrictive Practices Court has recently completed its passage through Parliament.

Despite these reservations it is generally agreed that the overall influence of the Court has been to free large areas of industry from the negative attitudes to competition, nourished during the depression of the inter-war period. Firms now have to think twice before initiating most forms of restrictive behaviour and this is particularly true, judging from past cases, of agreements involving, for example, quotas and aggregated rebates, that are likely to help maintain existing levels of concentration.

It is evident, therefore, that in the last decade British policy in this field has moved closer to the U.S.A. where a wide range of practices involving price fixing and market sharing have been *per se* illegal since some of the earlier cases brought under the Sherman Act. In addition the Clayton Act

(1914) spelt out in more detail practices which tended to lessen competition or create a monopoly, especially price discrimination and tying and exclusive dealing arrangements. As a result the relative freedom of American industry from restrictive agreements is generally regarded as one of the most substantial achievements of its anti-trust policy.

Conclusion

The recent development in the U.K. of a comprehensive system of investigation into a wide range of restrictive practices, with an implicit bias against restraints on competition, makes it likely that any potentially undesirable increases in market concentration in the future will come from mergers. A concentration increase achieved by the internal growth of some firms and in the face of effective competition seems less likely to be accompanied by inefficiency than where existing firms are allowed to form an amalgamation responsible for a large proportion of domestic output. Although it is true that mergers between smaller firms in an industry can help to increase competition by strengthening their position *vis-à-vis* larger rivals, and although the Monopolies Commission has been convinced that some mergers between already dominant firms would be in the public interest, especially when the market is viewed as world-wide rather than confined simply to Britain, two important factors should not be overlooked. Firstly, the amount of evidence on the economies of scale that can be achieved by large *firms* (as opposed to large plants) is very sparse, as was indicated in chapter 2, and what evidence there is tends to suggest that such economies are not universal throughout manufacturing industry nor significant in reducing costs. Generally speaking, however, these are the economies that might be expected from mergers between large firms. Secondly, anti-trust agencies have typically been hard pressed to find a satisfactory remedy for an industry dominated by one or two firms whose performance is judged 'bad' in most respects. Thus to avoid the emergence of high levels of concentration which may eventually have undesirable consequences it seems crucial that horizontal (and to a lesser extent vertical and conglomerate) mergers involving large firms should be subjected to far more rigorous inquiry than many at present receive in Britain.

References

ADELMAN, M. A. (1958), 'The measurement of industrial concentration', in Heflebower, R. B., and Stocking, G. W. (eds.), *Readings in Industrial Organization and Public Policy*, Irwin.

ALLEN, G. C. (1968), *Monopolies and Restrictive Practices*, Allen & Unwin.

ARMSTRONG, A., and SILBERSTON, A. (1965), 'Size of plant, size of enterprise and concentration in British manufacturing industry, 1935–58', *Journal of the Royal Statistical Society*, vol. 128, series A, part 3, pp. 395–420.

AMEY, L. R. (1964), 'Diversified manufacturing businesses', *Journal of the Royal Statistical Society*, vol. 127, series A, part 2, pp.251–90.

BAIN, J. S. (1951), 'Relation of profit rate to industry concentration: American manufacturing, 1936–40', *Quarterly Journal of Economics*, vol. 65, no. 3, pp. 293–324.

BAIN, J. S. (1956), *Barriers to New Competition*, Harvard University Press.

BAIN, J. S. (1966), *International Differences in Industrial Structure*, Yale University Press.

BAIN, J. S. (1968), *Industrial Organization*, 2nd edn, Wiley. Yale University Press.

BATES, J. A. (1964), *The Financing of Small Business*, Sweet & Maxwell.

BERLE, A. A., and MEANS, G. C. (1932), *The Modern Corporation and Private Property*, Macmillan.

BLAIR, J. M. (1948), 'Technology and size', *American Economic Review*, Papers and Proceedings, vol. 38, no. 2, pp. 121–52.

BLAIR, J. M. (1956), 'Statistical measures of concentration in business', *Bulletin of the Oxford University Institute of Statistics*, vol. 18, no. 4, pp. 351–72.

BOARD OF TRADE (1962), *Report on the Census of Production for 1958*, H.M.S.O., part 35, Table 12.

BOARD OF TRADE (1963), *Report on the Census of Distribution and Other Services, 1961*, H.M.S.O., part 14, Table 6.

CAVES, R. E. (ed.) (1968), *Britain's Economic Prospects*, The Brookings Institution and Allen & Unwin.

COLLINS, N. R., and PRESTON, L. E. (1961), 'The size structure of the largest industrial firms, 1909–1958', *American Economic Review*, vol. 51, no. 5, pp. 986–1011.

Company Assets, Income and Finance in 1960 (1962), H.M.S.O.

Company Assets, Income and Finance in 1963 (1965), H.M.S.O.

EDWARDS, C. D. (1964), '*Economic Concentration*', part 1 of Hearings before the Senate Subcommittee on Antitrust and Monopoly: *Overall and Conglomerate Aspects*, U.S. Govt. Printing Office.

EDWARDS, R. S., and TOWNSEND, H. (1958), *Business Enterprise*, Macmillan.

EVELY, R., and LITTLE, I. M. D. (1960), *Concentration in British Industry*, Cambridge University Press.

FLORENCE, P. S. (1961), *Ownership, Control and Success of Large Companies*, Sweet & Maxwell.

FREEMAN, C. (1962), 'Research and development: a comparison between British and American industry', *National Institute Economic Review*, no. 20, pp. 21–39.

FREEMAN, C. (1965), 'Research and development in electronic capital goods', *National Institute Economic Review*, no. 34, pp. 40–91.

GALBRAITH, J. K. (1963), *American Capitalism*, Penguin Books.

HART, P. E. (1960), 'Business concentration in the United Kingdom', *Journal of the Royal Statistical Society*, vol. 123, series A, part 1, pp. 50–58.

HART, P. E. (ed.) (1968), *Studies in Profit, Business Saving and Investment in the United Kingdom, 1920–62*, vol. 2, Allen & Unwin.

HART, P. E., and PRAIS, S. J. (1956), 'The analysis of business concentration: a statistical approach', *Journal of the Royal Statistical Society*, vol. 119, series A, part 2, pp. 150–81.

HEATH, J. B. (1961), 'Restrictive practices and after', *Manchester School of Economic and Social Research*, vol. 29, no. 2, pp. 173–202.

INLAND REVENUE (1963), *106th Report of the Commissioners*, H.M.S.O.

JEWKES, J., SAWYERS, D., and STILLERMAN, R. (1958), *The Sources of Invention*, Macmillan.

KAYSEN, C. (1961), 'The corporation: how much power? What scope?' in Mason, E. S. (ed.), *The Corporation in Modern Society*, Harvard University Press.

KAYSEN, C., and TURNER, D. F. (1959), *Antitrust Policy*, Harvard University Press.

MANN, H. M. (1966), 'Seller concentration, barriers to entry and rates of return in thirty industries, 1950–60', *Review of Economics and Statistics*, vol. 48, no. 3, pp. 296–307.

MANSFIELD, E. (1963), 'Size of firm, market structure and innovation', *Journal of Political Economy*, vol. 121, no. 6, pp. 556–76.

MANSFIELD, E. (1964), 'Industrial research and development expenditures', *Journal of Political Economy*, vol. 122, no. 4, pp. 319–40.

MARTIN, D. D. (1963), 'The Brown shoe case and the new anti-merger policy', *American Economic Review*, vol. 53, no. 3, pp. 340–58.

MASON, E. S. (1957), *Economic Concentration and the Monopoly Problem*, Harvard University Press.

MASON, E. S. (ed.) (1961), *The Corporation in Modern Society*, Harvard University Press.

MINISTRY OF AGRICULTURE (1967), *Agricultural Statistics, 1964–5*, H.M.S.O., Table 68.

MONOPOLIES COMMISSION (1952), *Report on the Supply of Insulated Electric Wires and Cables*, H.M.S.O.

MONOPOLIES COMMISSION (1954), *Report on the Process of Calico Printing*, H.M.S.O.

MONOPOLIES COMMISSION (1955), *Report on Collective Discrimination*, H.M.S.O.

MONOPOLIES COMMISSION (1956), *Report on the Supply of Certain Industrial and Medical Gases*, H.M.S.O.

MONOPOLIES COMMISSION (1956a), *Report on the Supply of Certain Rubber Footwear*, H.M.S.O.

MONOPOLIES COMMISSION (1961), *Report on the Supply of Cigarettes and Tobacco*, H.M.S.O.

MONOPOLIES COMMISSION (1966), *Report on Supply of Household Detergents*, H.M.S.O.

MONOPOLIES COMMISSION (1968), *Report on the Supply of Man-Made Cellulosic Fibres*, H.M.S.O.

MOODY, J. (1904), *The Truth about the Trusts*, Moody Publishing Co.

MUELLER, W. F. (1964), *Economic Concentration*, part 2 of Hearings before the Senate Subcommittee on Antitrust and Monopoly, U.S. Govt. Printing Office.

NATIONAL BUREAU OF ECONOMIC RESEARCH (1955), *Business Concentration and Price Policy*, Princeton University Press.

NATIONAL INSTITUTE OF ECONOMIC AND SOCIAL RESEARCH (1955), *A Classified List of Large Companies Engaged in British Industry*, N.I.E.S.R.

NATIONAL INSTITUTE OF ECONOMIC AND SOCIAL RESEARCH (1956), *Company Income and Finance, 1949–53*, N.I.E.S.R.

NELSON, R. L. (1959), *Merger Movements in American Industry, 1895–1956*, Princeton University Press.

PRATTEN, C. F. (1968), 'The merger boom in manufacturing industry', *Lloyds Bank Review*, October.

PRATTEN, C. F., and DEAN, R. M. (1965), *The Economies of Large-Scale Production in British Industry*, Cambridge University Press.

ROBINSON, E. A. G. (1959), *The Structure of Competitive Industry*, Nisbet.

ROSENBLUTH, G. (1955), 'Measures of concentration', in Stigler, G. J. (ed.), *Business Concentration and Price Policy*, Princeton University Press.

ROWLEY, C. K. (1966), *The British Monopolies Commission*, Allen & Unwin.

ROWLEY, C. K. (1968), 'Monopoly in Britain: private vice but public virtue?', *Moorgate and Wall Street*, Autumn.

SCHMOOKLER, J. S. (1959), 'Bigness, fewness and research', *Journal of Political Economy*, vol. 117, no. 6, pp. 628–32.

SHEPHERD, W. G. (1961), 'A comparison of industrial concentration in the United States and Britain', *Review of Economics and Statistics*, vol. 43, no. 1, pp. 70–75.

SILBERMAN, I. H. (1967), 'On lognormality as a summary measure of concentration', *American Economic Review*, vol. 107, no. 4, pp. 807–30.

SINGER, E. M. (1968), *Antitrust Economics*, Prentice-Hall.

STEVENS, R. B., and YAMEY, B. S. (1965), *The Restrictive Practices Court*, Weidenfeld & Nicolson.

STIGLER, G. J. (ed.) (1955), *Business Concentration and Price Policy*, Princeton University Press.

STIGLER, G. J. (1963), *Capital and Rates of Return in Manufacturing Industries*, Princeton University Press.

WEISS, L. W. (1961), *Economics and American Industry*, Wiley.

White Paper (1964), *Monopolies, Mergers and Restrictive Practices*, Cmnd 2299, H.M.S.O.

White Paper (1966), *Industrial Reorganization Corporation*, Cmnd 2889, H.M.S.O.

Index

Penguin Modern Economics Texts

A new series of short, original unit texts on various aspects of thought and research in important areas of economics. The series is under the general editorship of B. J. McCormick, Senior Lecturer in Economics, University of Sheffield.

Balance-of-Payments Policy
B. J. Cohen

The Control of the Money Supply
A. D. Bain

The Economics of Agriculture
David Metcalf

The Economics of the Common Market
D. Swann

Elements of Regional Economics
Harry W. Richardson

The International Monetary System
Herbert G. Grubel

Nationalized Industries
Graham L. Reid and Kevin Allen

The Principles of Development Aid
E. K. Hawkins

The Theory of Taxation
Charles M. Allan

Trade and Specialization
Ronald Findlay

Wages
B. J. McCormick

Penguin Modern Economics Readings

Economics of Education
vols. 1 and 2
Edited by M. Blaug

Economic Policy for Development
Edited by I. Livingstone

Economics of Technological Change
Edited by Nathan Rosenberg

Foreign Aid
Edited by Jagdish Bhagwati and Richard S. Eckaus

Growth Economics
Edited by Amartya Sen

Inflation
Edited by R. J. Ball and Peter Doyle

International Finance
Edited by R. N. Cooper

International Trade
Edited by Jagdish Bhagwati

The Labour Market
Edited by B. J. McCormick and E. Owen Smith

Managerial Economics
Edited by G. P. E. Clarkson

Monetary Theory
Edited by R. W. Clower

Monopoly and Competition
Edited by Alex Hunter

Power in Economics
Edited by K. W. Rothschild

Public Enterprise
Edited by R. Trovey

Public Finance
Edited by R. W. Houghton

Regional Analysis
Edited by L. Needleman

Transport
Edited by Denys Munby